Travels in the
World of Books

Travels in the World of Books

Nick Smith

RARE BOOKS AND BERRY

First published in 2010 by

Rare Books and Berry
High Street, Porlock,
Minehead, Somerset
TA24 8PU

www.rarebooksandberry.co.uk

© Nick Smith

A CIP catalogue record for this title is
Available from the British Library

ISBN 978-0-9563867-0-0

Designed and typeset in Minion at
Alacrity, Sandford, Somerset

Printed and bound by
The Cromwell Press Group, Wiltshire

For
Phil George
who started the adventures

Contents

Preface

By Michael Berry

Editor, *Bookdealer* magazine, 2007-10

A FEW YEARS AGO I bought *Bookdealer*, and overnight I became a magazine publisher and editor. As a seller of new and antiquarian books I found it all a bit of a daunting adventure. Up until that point *Bookdealer* had been a classified advertising, listings and lineage publication with the occasional piece of editorial dedicated to the inner workings of the trade. But the internet changed all that and, with so many on-line resources for book collectors, I decided that if I were to make a go of my new business venture I'd need to do something different with it.

I decided to commission reviews of new books, but I also felt that I needed a few regular columns to flesh it out for the reader. I phoned a journalist and magazine editor I'd worked with in the past – the award-wining Nick Smith – and asked him if he'd like to contribute on a regular basis. He immediately said yes, but then qualified this by adding that he knew 'next to nothing' about the book trade. Doesn't matter, I told him, and explained that I just wanted him to write original material about what books meant to him as a writer, a reader and a consumer.

And so the column 'Double Booked' was born and off Nick went to write it. I remember when the first episode turned up, containing one of his many swipes at the large book chain stores that irritate so many in the book trade. I liked it. It was informed, newsworthy and hard-hitting. Nick was a good spotter of 'the Emperor's new clothes' and seemed more than happy to slaughter the occasional sacred cow. There were no other literary columns I could think of that were of its sort and we agreed that, while the ideas kept coming, the column would keep running.

After about a year, just as 'Double Booked' was settling into a style that seemed to me to be perfect for the magazine, it all changed. Nick, who in his many newspaper and magazine assignments was increasingly visiting the most far-flung corners of the world, told me that what he really wanted to write about was travel and travel writing. I knew that he'd been a judge on the prestigious Thomas Cook Travel Book of the Year Award and agreed that he should.

The column grew an extra title and became known as 'More Travels in the World of Books'. At this point I felt sure that we were onto a winner and, as the articles became longer and longer, often accompanied by Nick's own superb photography, I started to think that they should be bundled up between a set of boards. What you have in your hands – *Travels in the World of Books* – is the result: a collection of columns that started out being about the book trade, with the occasional reference to the travel genre, but which gradually evolved into being decidedly more travel-oriented, with the occasional reference to the book trade. And none the worse for that.

You can't write a book like this unless you've read a lot of books and travelled many a mile. But what really impresses me is that, while most books need just one good idea to get them started, this needed many more – in fact at least one for every time *Bookdealer* went to press. To sustain this over a three-year period speaks volumes for the breadth and depth of Nick's reading, which never fails to astound me. Month after month, as I received his copy, quite often with only hours to spare, I'd phone Nick and simply say, 'I don't know how you do it.'

His answer was always the same: 'Oh it's easy, so long as you waste as much time as I do in hotels and airports.' But it wasn't wasted: while others squander their time and money in Duty Free shops and lobby bars, Nick read book after book and came up with thousands upon thousands of words. In the course of writing *Travels in the World of Books*, Nick's been from Namibia to the North Pole, Canada to China, Libya to Lithuania, Iran to Iceland, Egypt to Ecuador. I imagine that one of the most interesting books in his possession is his passport.

I've now come to the end of my editorship on *Bookdealer*, and as it passes into new hands I hope that my successor will continue with this quirky, learned and often very funny column. And I look forward to being invited to write the Preface for the second volume in a few years time.

May 2010

Acknowledgements

TRAVELS IN THE WORLD OF BOOKS could not have been written without the help of many people who kept me travelling and assisted with the text.

Mike Berry commissioned the column from the word go. Mick Herron read every word of it, month-in, month-out, prior to filing. *Bookdealer's* Jean Desebrock made sure that the copy was in shape for publication. At this point it's traditional to say that any remaining errors in the text are my own, but since all three have edited this book at least once I've no hesitation in blaming them.

Various editors have kept the writing and photography commissions coming in, and in doing so have provided me with the opportunity to travel to places I'd otherwise never have visited. So thanks to: Fiona Donald of the *Daily Telegraph*, Angela M.H. Schuster of the *Explorers Journal*, Carla Passino of *Country Life International*, Geordie Torr of *Geographical*, Dickon Ross of *Engineering and Technology*, Sean Blair of *Flipside* and Steve Watkins of *Outdoor Photography*.

No PR company has done more than BGB communications to keep me airborne, so thank you Hannah, Kath, Maitha, Pegi and Sara. Quark Expeditions got me to the North Pole by sea, while Omega Watches inadvertently provided some of the travel, as did Imagine Africa. Charlotte Bell of Campbell-Bell Communications made sure that there was often a bottle of Mumm Champagne in the mix, while Chris Edwards provided plenty of suggestions, IT support and Guinness.

Sir Christopher Ondaatje offered advice and encouragement, as did Alexander McCall Smith, Jenny Balfour Paul, Martin Hartley, John Hemming, Alexandra Shackleton and Shane and Nigel Winser.

Heartfelt thanks are due to Suzette who designed the cover, but more importantly gave me the time to read, write and travel. Also, to our wonderful little daughter Tigger, who tried every trick in the book to drag her Daddy to the park on those Sundays when he should have been writing.

List of photographs

15

Village Cigars in New York, taken on 15th January 2009, the day of the 'Miracle on the Hudson'. *(Chapter 22)*

Wide-angle 'floor shot' up a mature elephant's trunk. *(Chapter 25)*

Injured leopard in Botswana's Okavango Delta. Not a man-eater, but quite possibly as dangerous as those shot by Jim Corbett. *(Chapter 25)*

Neil Armstrong and Buzz Aldrin on the surface of the Moon during their *Apollo 11* expedition (posed by models). *(Chapter 27)*

The author at a ceremonial North Pole, a few miles away from 90 degrees north. *(Chapter 28)*   *Photo: Sue Flood*

Polar bear on the Arctic ice close to Franz Josef Land, Russia. *(Chapter 28)*

A bookshop inside the old railway station in Damascus in Syria, with strong associations with T.E. Lawrence and the Arab Revolt. *(Chapter 31)*

Journey's start and end. The beach at Jambiani in Zanzibar where the author started and finished his four-year trip around the world with the seafaring novels of Patrick O'Brian. *(Chapter 32)*

Part of a herd of more than a hundred elephants at Ol Malo, Northern Kenya. *(Chapter 35)*

'I had a farm in Africa at the foot of the Ngong Hills.' Karen Blixen's coffee farm in suburban Nairobi. *(Chapter 35)*

The compass that Shackleton took with him to his farthest South on the *Nimrod* expedition of 1907-09. *(Appendix 2)*

A note on the text

ALL OF THE PIECES in this book originally appeared in
Bookdealer magazine during the period 2007-10. Many of
the early episodes were written in response to specific
events: the publication of a new title, the collapse of a high
street chain, the announcement of a competition winner. As
a result, some of the columns are now hopelessly out of date
and, no matter what approach I took to editing them for
this collection, they have remained so. Hopefully, there's still
enough of interest in them to make the occasional revisit
not a complete waste of time, but the nature of bundled-up
journalism is sadly that some of what follows will be for
posterity and completists only. Later instalments that deal
more with my own travels and my response to the literature
of the regions have fared much better.

In the course of preparing the articles for *Travels in the
World of Books* I've stripped them of their journalistic stand-
firsts that might once have helped to put them in context.
This is because, for the most part, they're no longer helpful
and simply get in the way. Where some sort of context is
necessary, I've silently rewritten, added a footnote, or
credited the reader with the ability and inclination to eventually get the hang of what's going on.

I've also corrected as many of the errors and knocked out

as many infelicities as I could find, with the exception of 'The spy who franked me' which, if the central error were to be corrected, would fall apart.   *NS*

CHAPTER 1

The wine-dark sea

PERHAPS IT'S just me, but these days I get more of a thrill buying wine in my local supermarket than I do shopping for books in the big-name chains. For one thing, the wine racks of my local supermarket offer more choice, and at least I come away from Tesco or Sainsbury's or wherever thinking I've got reasonable value for money. Don't get me wrong: I don't think when I buy a perfectly ordinary Australian chardonnay at 'half price' that I'm getting a bargain. I don't think I'm a clever shopper and I doubt the wine will be much good either. But, I'm perfectly happy to accept that Tesco has done its homework, and knows that no matter how much I resist I'm going to cave in and buy what it wants me to buy. I put up with this because it's just a bottle of plonk, and at the end of the day I'll get home, put my feet up and quaff it with a damned good book.

Despite Tesco having a portfolio of about a hundred book titles on offer most people prefer to go to a bookshop on their local high street to buy their 'damned good book', though it is becoming increasingly unclear why. The big

19

chains on Tottenham Court Road, Oxford Street and Piccadilly hardly justify the trip into Town. And although it pains me to admit it, deep down I know that the purpose of the modern bookstore is the same as the supermarket. Its express intention is to part you from as much of your hard-earned cash as possible in as short a time as possible, while delivering as big a return to its shareholders as possible. We can hardly blame the likes of Waterstone's and Borders for wanting to cash in on an emerging science that another, significantly bigger market sector has invested in so heavily. But it's all so depressingly blatant.

Store managers in the book trade have pilfered from the food retail sector the hard-won conclusion that you can sell pretty much anything so long as it's near the till, has perceived 'added value', or is discounted. Although I don't have the exact figures to hand, I imagine my contact in the trade was not far wrong when he estimated 'ninety per cent of the modern chain bookshop's revenue is generated from ten per cent of its floor-space'. This fertile area will be near the main entrance and will be densely packed with three types of book: those on bestsellers lists, those signed by the author and those included in an array of offers ranging from 'three-for-two' to the blunter buy-one-get-one-frees. (Hats off incidentally to the independent that recently introduced a 'two-for-three' offer, where you take three books to the counter and they'll tell you which one not to bother with. They're also offering the latest Harry Potter at a penny off.).

Now, I'm not against having all these heavily promoted volumes thrust in my face, and neither do I care that publishers waste money promoting their indifferent books.

But I do hate it that the once pleasurable experience of *browsing* for books has mutated into *shopping* for them. Take the case of a typical casual punter, John Smith, who in his innocence buys a chart-topping ghost-written auto-biography of a footballer (it's a present for his father), a signed copy of a novel set in Botswana for his mother, and three paperbacks (for the price of two) to read on his forthcoming holiday. He takes them to the counter, pleased with having got everything done in minutes, along with saving some money and acquiring the autograph of a leading author.

So far so good, but at what point does the bookstore feel that it should point out to John Smith that he's being, if not deceived, then at the very least manipulated? Where is the 'Government Health Warning' saying that these signed editions may not be firsts and, in investment terms, are almost certainly worthless? (Even if we were to assume the average punter isn't buying them as an investment, it's fair to assume that the seller isn't doing that much to disabuse the less experienced buyer of the impression that these books are somehow 'special' or 'collectable'). Where does it say that chart-topping books have less to do with the ebb and flow of the public's literary taste and more to do with what the publishers are taking a punt on this season? The answer is 'nowhere.' But by this point John Smith is on his mobile in the Samuel Pepys in Mayfair, telling everyone that shopping for books has never been easier.

Let's assume that this happens on a daily basis (and it must do, because these bear-trap displays are becoming endemic). The predictable course of events is that fewer titles will be relied on to generate revenue for the business, worse books will necessarily become even more heavily backed and the stores themselves will have to protect their income by diversifying into selling DVDs and opening up coffee bars (and maybe even start stocking wine?) And while the casual punter may be blissfully unaware of all this, he'll at some point find himself wishing that there was more variety from which to choose. He may even perhaps recall the halcyon days when you could go into a bookshop – the days when they were free from the all-pervasive smell of coffee and the irritation of piped muzak – and buy what you actually wanted rather than what you are told to want. I know that this is the nature of the modern world, but at least with wine, if you find something half-decent at a reasonable price near the till you can stock up and keep on drinking it when the offer closes. But with books one good read will have to lead to another.

In the original draft of this article I took great pains to point out my belief that the half-price wine offers in high street supermarkets were boloney on the basis that the original prices had been hyper-inflated to allow for the advertised depth of discount. I further claimed that by the time the prices had been fixed you were paying pretty much the market value of the bottle, while being left with the impression that you'd cannily snaffled a bargain.

I withdrew the accusation pre-press after being warned by a consumer journalist friend that supermarket chains are notoriously litigious and would almost certainly sue me if I said anything ungentlemanly about what I believe to be their dastardly marketing schemes that are evil covert attempts at deception. As I write this note there is a line of St Emilion in my local supermarket going at around seven quid a bottle. Half price. The only question you have to ask yourself is would you pay fourteen quid for the bottle? And the answer is, 'no, I wouldn't.' It's rubbish. As the computer manufacturer said to the record company: 'sosumi'.

Meanwhile, the Samuel Pepys pub on Clarges Street in Mayfair has changed its name to the slightly less literary, and distinctly more agricultural, The Field.

CHAPTER 2

The man on the Clapham omnibus

MAYBE THE *Daily Telegraph* was short on news, but a few weeks ago 'the last of the broadsheets' gave a whopping 16 column inches to a PR puff from Waterstone's announcing yet another chart of the Nation's favourite books. With a numerological neatness that might have impressed the great John Milton himself, this time it was the top 25 books published in the past 25 years, by way of celebrating 25 years of Waterstone's presence on the High Street. On the face of it, a fairly harmless stunt plucked out of the air for a bit of 'feel good' exposure. But, as we shall see, there were Machiavellian doings afoot and not all was as it seemed.

The way the poll worked was that Waterstone's staff compiled a list of one hundred of the best reads published in the past quarter of a century that was then whittled down to a final 25 by thousands of the reading public. I'm not quite sure who this public is, but with J.K. Rowling's *Harry*

Potter and the Philosopher's Stone topping the chart ahead of
Umberto Eco's *The Name of the Rose,* I can only assume that
it is the same public that always votes for J.R.R. Tolkien's *The
Lord of the Rings* as 'the best book ever in the history of book
publishing ever' (or whatever).

Let's have a look at what's in the top 25. A quick scan
down the list shows a fairly even split between literary
fiction (Sebastian Faulks's *Birdsong*), airport novels (Dan
Brown's *The Da Vinci Code*), children's allegory (Philip
Pullman's *Northern Lights*) and a few travel favourites
written to be read while commuting to work on the Underground, such as Bill Bryson's *Notes from a Small Island.*
A foot in every camp then, with pretty much every title so
far either a blockbuster movie, a future blockbuster movie
or a big hit on terrestrial TV.

I'm not joking. Closer inspection reveals that at least
60 per cent of the shortlist has been televised or made into
a film (with the remainder presumably in production or
option-tied). This doesn't reveal anything too spectacular,
because it stands to reason that popular books make
popular visual entertainment (although my sources in the
movie world tell me that *Northern Lights* will have to lose a
lot of its atheist message in the final cut, if it's to go national
in the United States). Likewise, you can't blame members of
the public for enjoying a movie so much that they want to
find out what the real thing is all about. You could argue
that the main reason Austen, Dickens and Thackeray are
read on the Clapham omnibus today is because they have
been discovered by the reader after watching a costume
drama either on the TV or at the Ritzy.

Even closer inspection of the Waterstone's top 25 reveals that nearly all the titles are on another list, a list that I put together in five minutes after searching the internet using the term 'popular book club books'. So the picture emerges that just about every book on Waterstone's list is there because we have either seen the movie or we have been told to read it by someone with a vested interest in promoting it. In terms of digestibility, they're all frighteningly easy to read while appearing to be highbrow, middle class and culturally significant. There are no wild cards on the list, so there's no need to feel inadequate. The list also cleverly takes into account that the British public tends to get very defensive about long books, often confusing the fact that they have actually finished one with it being any good (Louis de Bernières' *Captain Corelli's Mandolin*).

I don't want to pick on J.K. Rowling, but hands up anyone who seriously thinks *Harry Potter and the Philosopher's Stone* is a better book, a more deserving winner of such a poll, than, say, J.M. Coetzee's *Disgrace*, Martin Amis's *Money*, Ian McEwan's *Atonement*, Kazuo Ishiguro's *The Remains of the Day* or A.S. Byatt's *Possession: A Romance*. None of these is on the Waterstone's list, presumably because the staff that compiled the original, from which the shortlist is derived, find works of genuine cultural significance a little more difficult to read. Enter Waterstone's spokesman Jon Howells, who told the *Daily Telegraph*, 'I think it's a justified winner.'

Maybe it's just not in Waterstone's interest to plug such comparatively worthy titles. After all, they won't sell as well as, say, Arthur Golden's *Memoirs of a Geisha* or Kate Mosse's

Labyrinth, no matter how hard they are plugged. And as with many High Street chains, Waterstone's is desperately short on sales, so they need to roll out the gimmicks. Hence yet another bloody list.

What the *Daily Telegraph* is doing publishing such froth I don't know, when there is the actual news that Waterstone's flagship supermarket at 311 Oxford Street is to close after only three years (as picked up in 4 column inches in 'Books & Bookmen' in *Private Eye*). The closure of the Oxford Street shop is the eighth such for Waterstone's in 2007, with more reportedly in the pipeline. So you can see why, from the retailer's point of view, a nice fluffy reader poll in the *Telegraph* couldn't have been better timed. It was 'a good day to bury news'.

Maybe I'm taking this all a bit too seriously. After all, polls like this are only supposed to be a bit of fun. But even so, there should be more clarity. We should come clean and admit that at their best they're unscientific, while at their worst they provide free advertisements in the national newspapers for ailing retailers. If we truly want to know what the best – or even the best loved – books are, we should conduct such experiments independently, with at least some attempt at objectivity. Having said that, in the music industry, where I did a stint as a cub reporter, they've been trying to pinpoint the best album for years. No matter how expertly the poll is conducted, it's always the Beatles' *Abbey Road* and the Beach Boys' *Pet Sounds* that win. The only conclusion I can draw from this is that, when it comes to popular music, the British public will not deviate from the received orthodoxy, preferring polished mediocrity to

27

genuine greatness. And if the recent Waterstone's poll is anything to go by, it's exactly the same in the world of books.

At the time of going to press plans for completing the film trilogy of His Dark Materials *have been shelved in the United States after an avalanche of protests from the Christian right.*

CHAPTER 3

Key signatures

A THRILLER-WRITING friend of mine once told me over a drink in the Dickens in Paddington that, while he was extremely pleased that a chain bookseller in Clapham was prominently displaying his new paperback, they simply weren't moving off the shelves. 'If only I had the time to go and sign them,' he sighed, idly completing the *Telegraph* crossword, 'they'd stand more chance of selling.' I thought about this for a moment and then I hit the jackpot. 'Look,' I said. 'I live quite near Clapham. I'll pop in and sign them for you. Just give me something with your name on in case I need to identify myself.'

I'm not going to reveal how much we'd had to drink that night, but at the time the plan seemed watertight. My friend isn't yet well known outside the genre and his portrait never appears on his book jackets, so what was there to prevent me inscribing his books for him? A few days later I walked into the store with my fake ID, smiled sweetly at the student behind the counter, and asked if I could sign that pile of books over there? No problem, sir, come this way. A few moments later, the job was done. No, I made that last bit up. I couldn't go through with it: the deception would be too great. But it did get me thinking about our obsession with signed books.

The reason publishers and booksellers encourage authors to sign their books today is simply to make them more attractive, collectable or valuable to the book-buying public. In a way they might be right, but it's a bit of a scam because signatures on new books rarely do little more than deface them. And so it's something of a twist of fate that personalising a printed book with the author's signature has its roots in an early form of counter-piracy measure. I learned this from my tutor at Oxford, the venerable Dr Roger Lonsdale, an authority on the Augustan period and editor of the *New Oxford Book of 18th Century Verse*. I was testing my rather absurd theory that Laurence Sterne's *Tristram Shandy* was the original modern novel, and that Salman Rushdie had pinched its structure for *Midnight's Children*, when I realised that my English tutor's attention had drifted to a higher plane.

After a moment or two Dr Lonsdale lit up a Silk Cut and reached for a volume of an early edition of *Shandy*, scruffy in its leather binding and not very modern looking. I opened it carefully to find Sterne's signature on the title-page. 'Ah,' said the good Doctor, 'how I wish it weren't signed. Then it really would be worth something.' He then explained how Sterne was plagued by fraudulent imitators. John Carr produced a fake third volume in 1760, while J. Hall-Stevenson and Richard Griffiths unashamedly wrote 'posthumous' continuations of both *Tristram Shandy* and

A Sentimental Journey after Sterne's death in 1768. Dr Lonsdale explained that Sterne would literally 'authorise' editions of his books by standing in the bindery and autographing them for his publisher, who would then advertise to his clients that the only authentic versions were those signed by the man himself. Ever since hearing this story – and I'm prepared to admit it's not necessarily the *only* origin of why books are signed by their author – I've been attracted to the idea that the signature on a book behaves in the way a signature works on a cheque. In other words, it's a thing of the past and there's no real need for it now.

Even so, these days you can't move for authors scribbling all over their latest publications. And while we may wish to put this down to, perhaps, a harmless moment of vanity on the writer's part – I certainly intend to sign every copy of *Travels in the World of Books* whether the purchasers want me to or not – there is also something more sinister going on. There's a thriving scam similar to ticket touting operating on the internet where cyber squatters, who are not bona fide dealers, snap up potentially collectable books in vast quantities before flogging them on eBay. This happened recently when Hatchards offered its e-mail database signed copies of Seamus Heaney's *District and Circle* through an e-alert. The following day these books were going for ten times their cover price on eBay. And although I don't as a rule have much sympathy with publishing houses I can understand how this activity could get right up their noses. As a result of what is effectively a black market, some authors have become reluctant to sign altogether. Although I don't much like her books, I do respect J.K. Rowling for hardly signing anything at all these days – the mere act only makes money for third parties, and is a pretty extravagant example of the law of diminishing returns in meltdown. The almost supernaturally broke Dylan Thomas understood this well and worked the system to his advantage. The Welsh poet routinely settled his bar tabs with a cheque, certain that most of his cheques would remain uncashed and kept as souvenirs that with time might increase in value and be attractive to ephemera collectors.

But it's not just me who thinks collecting modern signed editions as an investment is a bit of a waste of time. A bookseller I know in Cecil Court told me that he had no idea why the majority of authors sign books today, since in most cases the signature adds neither rarity nor value to the book. He went on to say that it's a yardstick of his that, unless the author is a particularly rare signer, then a signature on the title-page post-1960 is almost meaningless. On the other hand it's hard to deny that a signed copy of a book can be a terrific memento of attending a reading by an important literary figure. I certainly enjoyed meeting the likes of William Golding, Anthony Burgess and Ted Hughes, while my signed copy of Auden's *Letters from Iceland* puts me directly in touch with a generation only just before mine, yet somehow completely out of reach.

Of course I go to book signings because, whether or not a contemporary writer's autograph means anything in commercial terms, it's always nice to meet a poet or a novelist. I remember very well a reading by one of my all-time favourites, Tony Harrison. He was reading in Blackwell's on Broad Street back when it used to be worth going there, and at the end we all formed a queue for the great man to sign our books. Perhaps there is something uncomplicated about the northern poet, but instead of signing my copy of *The School of Eloquence* he merely struck out his name on the title-page with a violent and squiggly line, while grunting the word 'Aye.' Now that's personal.

I recently attended the launch of A Chronology of Antarctic Exploration: A Synopsis of Events and Activities from the Earliest Times until the International Polar Years, 2007-09, *by the worthy Robert Keith Headland, formerly of the Scott Polar Research Institute in Cambridge. There was a swanky do at New Zealand House with plenty of book-launch wine and, as I picked up my copy, the author, who was in a convivial mood, asked me if I'd like him to sign it, or would I prefer a much rarer unsigned copy? The old ones are indeed the best.*

CHAPTER 4

Harry Potter and the predictable anticlimax

POOR J.K. ROWLING. She can't win. A decade ago she was the great new talent in children's literature: her books met with universal critical acclaim and she could do no wrong. Her PR machine caught onto the fact that she had a tabloid-friendly rags-to-riches story to go with it, and before long she was being romanticised in the redtops. Fleet Street had a field day drooling over a dishy single mother, her puking and mewling infant at her side, as she scribbled away in dank cafes in Edinburgh, writing stories that would make her richer than the Queen.

Today the same newspapers accuse her of cashing in on the Harry Potter phenomenon that she created, while the same critics pan her books. The movie, merchandising and marketing rollercoaster has gone off the rails, and the only thing we can say with any certainty is that the book series has come to a welcome end. Rowling made this abundantly clear when she slapped an epilogue on the seventh and final volume, *Harry Potter and the Deathly Hallows*, stating in unequivocal terms that they all lived happily ever after, or something like that.

It would come as no surprise to hear she was glad to see the back of it all. The series degenerated from being a joy to read at the start to a downright chore at the end. While her storytelling and powers of invention can be quite gifted, her prose is never much better than colourless, and by the end it was awful. It was almost as if she came to *dislike* the process of writing, her careful plots deteriorating into clunky shunting from A to B without appearing to care much how.

But the big question is *why*? Why have her books, after showing so much promise, tailed off in quality so dramatically? Part of the answer perhaps lies in the structure of the series, where each volume represents a year in the school career of the protagonist Harry. This means that unlike, say, Biggles or the Baudelaires in the *Lemony Snicket* series, there is a requirement for our central character to develop with time and even grow up. And while Rowling may have a talent for depicting 11-year-old wizards, when it comes to loathsome teenage oiks she is terrible. Yet there was absolutely no need for her to commit to such a constricting literary device. *The Simpsons* has been in production for two decades now and no one would ever want or expect Bart to grow up.

There are two distinct phases in the Harry Potter heptalogy: firstly there are the 'Thin Harries', the opening three books in the series, being *The Philosopher's Stone*, *The Chamber of Secrets* and *The Prisoner of Azkaban*. These average roughly 300 pages, are tightly plotted and crisply written with neat little temporal tentacles reaching back and forth around the wider narrative. Then there are the final four books – the 'Fat Harries', being *The Goblet of Fire*, *The Order of the Phoenix*, *The Half-Blood Prince* and finally *The Deathly Hallows*. These tomes are so long that they are virtually cubic. None is shorter than 600 pages, while the longest of them (at more than 900) broke all records by becoming the longest children's book in print, mysteriously overtaking *The Lord of the Rings*, which at 1,066 pages appears to me at least to be longer, although the issue might be whether J.R.R. Tolkien's behemoth is one or three books.

I like the Thin Harries. In fact I think they're great. Not as great maybe as C.S. Lewis's *Narnia* heptateuch or Philip Pullman's *His Dark Materials* trilogy or even Ursula Le Guin's *Earthsea* trilogy (which recently mutated into a tetralogy), but they are in the same league as some of the best children's books of the 20th century. In particular, *The Prisoner of Azkaban* is bordering on being a masterpiece. When I reviewed it for a magazine in the late 1990s I described a 'denouement as intricate and as satisfactory as the close of a Mozart symphony'. This was all rather too florid for the boring sub-editor, who hacked my review to bits, but it does give you the idea that, broadly speaking, I have in the past been on Rowling's side.

The appeal of the Thin Harries is of course that they are about magic and wizards. Where Rowling excels, as with the very best children's authors, is in her ability to give an authentic account of a world that does not exist. In other words, she makes us care about what it's like to be a wizard dealing with magic on an everyday basis. But then she made her mistake. At the start of the Fat Harries she decided to become more interested in teenagers, *Adrian Mole*-style growing pains, difficulties with girls and trying to be cool (some of her 'down with the kids' dialogue is excruciating). The thing is, we've all been teenagers and we all know how unpleasant and dull it can be, but very few of us have been wizards, so please tell us more. Either she ran out of steam or inspiration, but by *The Deathly Hallows* she's even taking the magic for granted, which is one of the reasons Rowling's critics have been left feeling that she's bitten the hand that feeds.

Although it has now passed into conventional wisdom that the quality of Rowling's books is inversely proportional to their size, the Fat Harries aren't *all* bad. It was Tolkien who famously said in defence of his monster-work that 'the tale grew in the telling', and there's clearly something similar going on with Rowling. As with the old Oxford don, if nothing else she knows how to tell a rattling good story. You could argue that, the more the stories sprawl, the mythologies grow and the sub-creations take on lives of their own, the more the obsessive-compulsive end of the teen market, more used to computer role-playing games, will enjoy them.

Talking of digital technology, let's not forget that, in the age of PlayStation, the internet, iPods and mobile phones, hardly any kids read books at all these days, and even fewer read long ones. So for Rowling to get the nation's hooded and knife-wielding youth reading again qualifies her, in my book at least, for a gold medal.

CHAPTER 5

Conventional Wisden

YOU CAN TELL when it's all gone a bit quiet out in the middle because the radio commentary becomes more interesting. Last Saturday, as England eventually made light of a modest target set by India at Lord's to secure the NatWest one-day international series, Aggers, Blowers and the rest of the team were in full flow. There was plenty of the usual stuff about Dundee cakes, solitary pigeons, Father Time and so on. But then an extraordinary exchange, so remarkable that I wrote it down. It went something like this:

Commentator 1: I've heard that the 1926 edition of Wisden
has just been produced in facsimile...
Commentator 2: Why?
Commentator 1: Because it's good for collectors.

And that seemed sufficient for all present, as if we should all know why 'it's good for collectors'. Before long the commentators were happily discussing the relative merits of various north London curry houses, aeroplanes on their way to Heathrow and England's chances on their winter tour. No further word on the lemon-spined Cricketers' Almanack was uttered.

One of the great things about Wisden is that building a collection is pretty much open to anyone (it's a rare Wisden indeed that commands more than £1,000), but even so I felt excluded by this comment. I wanted to ask Commentator 1 if 1926 is a difficult year to get hold of. Is there a huge demand for it? Is it part of a series of facsimiles? Do collectors really want facsimiles? I was intrigued, feeling almost as baffled as the world's greatest batsman Sachin Tendulkar must have been when, at Trent Bridge in 2002, England skipper Michael Vaughan removed him with one of his occasional off-breaks.

It seems that the 1926 edition, despite being something of a classic, is of no particular financial value: decent copies are widely available for under £200. Perhaps aficionados will note that it's the first edition under the editorship of C. Stewart Caine. Those interested in records (and that must be pretty much the entire Wisden congregation) might smile knowingly at the fact that at 1,031 pages it was also the largest edition so far. The real connoisseur will already know that this was the fourth (and so far final) time that the 'Five Cricketers of the Year' section was dropped in order to make room for an extended special profile of one player, Jack Hobbs. This was in recognition of the Surrey man's overtaking W.G. Grace as the most prolific century-maker of all time. But there's nothing that I can see to warrant a special facsimile edition – unlike, say, some of the wartime editions, where paper restrictions mean that they have become very scarce.

Of course, in those days the Wisden Cricketers' Almanack didn't look as we're used to seeing it these days (although in recent years there's been a tragic deterioration in cover quality, as we shall see). The classic woodcut by Eric Ravilious of the two Victorian gentlemen playing in top hats – much as Flashman must have worn in *Flashman's Lady* – didn't appear until 1938. This was the year when the longest-running sporting annual, seemingly in serious decline, called in the image-makers to help increase sales – a process that can't have been helped much by the advent of the Second World War, which effectively put an end to the sport on any serious level until 1946. Even had the game continued, there would have been precious few test grounds available to play on: during the war Lord's was bombed, the Oval became a prisoner of war camp, and Old Trafford was home to a field hospital.

Ravilious remained on the cover of the almanack until 2003, when a photograph of Michael Vaughan temporarily replaced it. What was clearly meant as an honour to the highly successful Vaughan was somewhat undermined by the sheer tackiness of the design and the sliminess of the gesture. And what was so alarming about this incident was the way in which the editors had so comprehensively failed to grasp what made Wisden (and by logical extension, cricket itself) so special. Wisden without Ravilious is like *The Wind in the Willows* without E.H. Shepard, *The Lion, the Witch and the Wardrobe* without Pauline Baynes, or *Alice in Wonderland* without Sir John Tenniel. Not surprisingly, the masses revolted, and many (including myself) took up Wisden's rather lame offer to 'readers who prefer the traditional cover' to order a hastily put together replacement (including Ravilious) for free. To this day my copy of 140th Edition of Wisden is clothed in two dust-wrappers – the offending photographic jacket tucked away inside, while strap-lines on the traditional cover promise a tantalising selection of essays, including one entitled 'Don't Marry a Cricketer', further explained by the sub-strap, 'Derek Pringle on whether top players can be family men'.

But I digress. The damage was done and more was in store when, the following year, Editor Matthew Engel put two Australians (Ricky Ponting and Steve Waugh) on the cover, while demanding £2.50 from readers preferring a 'traditional cover'. I don't know if Ravilious has been reinstated and I don't much care: the Golden Age of Wisden was over and this was the last edition I ever bought. And it wasn't just a reaction to the editors thinking they knew better than their readers either. Thanks largely to online statistical resources such as Cricinfo (which Wisden owned until ESPN took it over), and the fact that these days the season never truly ends, the need for an annual product is diminishing.

Earlier this summer I took a stroll down to the Oval to watch England against India. During the luncheon interval I decided to pay a visit to the Surrey County Cricket Club library right at the top of the old pavilion. 'Library' is perhaps too grand a term for this small archive that seems hardly used, but it is a goldmine of information. In particular, there is a section of Wisdens going back to the 1860s, when of course it was called *The Cricketer's Almanack*. (That's not a misprint, the apostrophe metathesised to the right of the 's' after the fifth year.) As you might expect, much can be learned by merely looking at them, something akin to examining growth rings in a tree. Times of austerity mean thin, badly produced volumes, while years of prosperity have produced healthy buttercup yellow tomes several inches thick.

The Golden Age of English cricket came to an abrupt end when the Great War loomed on the horizon. Surrey called off their last two matches without being asked to forfeit their place at the top of the league, and so in 1914 won the title for the first time since 1899. The County Championship was then suspended from 1915 to 1918, and the Wisdens grew thinner and thinner, often being little more than an honour roll of cricketing men who had lost their lives in defence of their country. W.G. Grace famously shook his fist at the Zeppelins that flew over his south London home, while in the Long Room a memorial to the men of Surrey who lost their lives in the wars simply states, 'they played the game'. Indeed they did.

CHAPTER 6

Books do furnish a room

A FEW WEEKS AGO I was in the Old Bookbinders pub
in Oxford's Jericho having a pint with an old geo-
grapher friend of mine. Talk turned on climate
change, desert encroachment, food security in the Third
World and other global issues, but before long we'd landed
on the really important stuff and were debating the old
chestnut of whether you can have too many books. He's a
keen bookman, with one of the best private libraries of
travel and exploration literature that I know of.

After more than three decades of dedicated collecting, he
has accumulated firsts of every important book in the genre
in English, from the usual stuff by Eric Newby, Patrick Leigh
Fermor, Paul Theroux and Jonathan Raban to the really
serious collectors' items by Wilfred Thesiger, Gavin Young,
Gavin Maxwell, Peter Hopkirk ('required reading'), Francis
Younghusband, Peter Fleming and so on. What's more, most
of them are signed by the author, because he'd made a point
over the years of attending virtually every Monday night
lecture at the Royal Geographical Society. There can't be a

decent travel journalist alive who's not at some point delivered a talk at this wonderful lecture theatre and for anyone looking to get their firsts inscribed by the new generation of travel writers and explorers this is a happy hunting ground indeed. 'Of course,' he said, 'now that the children have gone to university and we've moved to a smaller house, there doesn't seem to be much room for my books these days.'

I sympathise. It has long been the procedure at Smith Towers that if you wish to add a book you must remove one to make room for it. Once upon a time this seemed a fine idea. A staunch believer in Sturgeon's Law ('ninety per cent of everything is crud') I saw it as the ideal opportunity to fine-tune my collection and introduce volumes of more enduring appeal. Sneakily hoping to buck the system, I duly took occasional boxes of worthless slim paperbacks to the charity shop on Streatham High Road and replaced them one-for-one with colossal photographic travel monographs, early 20th-century atlases and some big dictionaries (including for a reason that eludes me still one of Canadian English). But, I told myself, I was sticking to the rules and it was a game I was winning. I was tossing out the dog-eared Penguins I'd bought as an undergraduate and bringing in classic volumes of real substance that would be the keystones of my library for decades to come.

It's an unpalatable truth, but most books in most collections are not worth keeping and need to be thrown out to make room for more important ones. My problem was that after a while I simply couldn't jettison any more. There always seemed to be some niggling emotional attachment that stayed my hand. This Penguin copy of *Under Milk Wood* had been a birthday present from a girl whose name I can't remember, my *Complete Poems of Christina Rossetti* used to belong to a friend who died many years ago, this copy of *The Divine Comedy* is my only parallel text.

Also, throwing out paperbacks simply because they were paperbacks seemed to be bad thinking. I know that's what *everybody* does, but there were reasons why I didn't want to throw out my Foresters, Wodehouses and O'Brians. I read *The Ionian Mission* in Zanzibar, *Laughing Gas* in Mexico City and *Hornblower in the West Indies* while stuck in an airport in Madrid on an aborted expedition to Easter Island. The paperbacks stacked in my hallway say more about who I am and where I've been than the pristine hardbacks lovingly preserved in beautiful lime-wood bookcases in my living room. They have boarding passes tucked into them from long-forgotten trips that come alive again the minute I pick them up. I've never been afraid to jot all over paperbacks, and so they're packed with scribbled foreign phrases, currency conversions, overheard conversations and plots of novels I'll never write that seemed like a good idea at the time. Oscar Wilde's apophthegm about price and worth never seemed more appropriate.

Back in the Old Bookbinders my friend was warming to his theme. It seems that the problem of accommodating his ever-growing library in a series of houses of ever-decreasing size has not been helped by a wife who regards the steady accretion of books as unbefitting a balanced mind. I've met her many times and have often been struck by her delightful, intelligent and extraordinarily charming personality. So to hear such nonsense set me flat aback. After close questioning my friend revealed that his wife claims to have travelled the world in her youth with only a few paperbacks in her rucksack. These she swapped with other travellers, and so read dozens of books on the road, while never having more than a few hundred pages on her at any one time. As someone who's been known to post books home from China rather than leave any behind, by this stage I was feeling slightly faint and so scurried off to the bar for more beer.

I didn't think so at the time, but it pains me now to admit my friend's wife might have had a point. Although Anthony Powell is probably correct in that books really do furnish a room, I've now reached the point where for the sake of everyone's sanity I could do with making some space. The box room at the back of my house that I grandly call my study is so packed with books that there are days when I virtually have to dynamite my way to my desk. This rag-and-bone shop of dead trees that meets me on a Monday morning often reminds me of a chapter in Dylan Thomas's little-read novel *Adventures in the Skin Trade* entitled simply 'Plenty of Furniture', in which, at the height of his often forgotten comic powers, the Welshman describes a forest of tables, chairs, desks and so on.

For the moral of this tale perhaps we should turn to the General Prologue of *The Canterbury Tales*, whose Clerke of Oxenforde has at his bedside 'twenty bookes, clad in blak and reed'. Despite the Clerke's impoverishment, this was considered at the time to be plenty of books. Maybe as a former Clerke of Oxenforde myself, I should emulate my forebear and stick to a score of bedside books. That *was* what Chaucer meant, wasn't it?

46

CHAPTER 7

The spy who franked me

I N WHAT'S little more than the most cynical of extortions, the Royal Mail has announced the issue of a set of commemorative stamps to mark the publication of the seventh and final instalment of the Harry Potter series. Since I no longer have the press notice to hand, I can't be sure if we're supposed to be celebrating J.K. Rowling finishing the series, or that she's going to inflict no further volumes upon us. Unkind though this may be, one thing is sure, and that is it's a rare bandwagon that rolls past the marketers at the Royal Mail without someone leaping onto it.

Time was when 'commems' really were that, and, as with civic honours, only the great and the good ever came to be immortalised in such fashion. But not so today: my sources in the philatelic establishment tell me that the clever money is on a set of Narnia commems in 2008 timed to coincide with the release of the second movie in the series, *Prince Caspian*. Although this is not yet confirmed, the Royal Mail's counterpart in New Zealand has already made its announcement to that effect. Commemorating an author of note I can understand, but to roll out the red carpet for a movie adaptation of a single work seems to be taking things just a step too far.

The forthcoming release of a set marking the 100th anniversary of Ian Fleming's birth is therefore something of a break with recent trends. How nice that our favourite spy – James Bond, 007, licence to kill – is now taking a break from delivering memorable one-liners and helping to deliver the mail (always assuming that it's not backed up in a Belfast sorting office because of a wildcat postal workers' strike).

'On Her Majesty's postal service' was how the *Daily Telegraph* broke the news to its readers, before reminding us that Fleming's 14 Bond novels have sold more than 100 million copies worldwide (approximately three times more than the Harry Potter franchise). Of the 14, only six are represented, although the covers of three different editions of each title will appear on each stamp, making them something of a delight for Fleming aficionados. For the record they are: *Casino Royale, Dr No, Goldfinger, Diamonds Are Forever, For Your Eyes Only* and *From Russia With Love*. The *Telegraph* doesn't make clear what the selection criteria were, though it might be safe to suppose they were not picked on the merits of their theme tunes. Had they been, I'd wag the finger at the Royal Mail over the omission of *Live and Let Die*, the cover version of the theme tune of which, if you see what I mean, by Guns N' Roses, was, if I may borrow the epithet from Bertie Wooster, a pipterino.

Despite the Royal Mail issuing evermore sets of 'specials'

– more than a billion individual commemorative stamps get printed every year – the inclusion of a literary author on a stamp is still something of a rarity. Indeed, ever since the first postage stamp was issued in 1840, very few giants of the canon have made an appearance (although you could argue that Queen Victoria, whose face adorns the Penny Black, was a published diarist and as such we can trace a literary connection back to the word go). The Bard himself had to wait until 1964, when he was commemorated in a set issued to mark the Shakespeare Festival (he appeared again indirectly in 1995 when the Royal Mail celebrated the reopening of the Globe Theatre on the South Bank). The 1964 set comprised a 3d stamp showing Puck and Bottom from *A Midsummer Night's Dream*; a 6d with Feste from *Twelfth Night*; a 1/3d with the balcony scene from *Romeo and Juliet*, while on the 1/6d there is Henry V knelt in prayer. It was all a bit different then.

Robert Burns followed swiftly in 1966, while the 1970s saw John Keats and Sir Walter Scott gracing the top right-hand corner of our envelopes. In the 1980s the Royal Mail honoured the Brontës, George Eliot and Edward Lear, while in the 1990s Thomas Hardy, Lord Tennyson and T.S. Eliot joined the select band. Before we start strewing laurels at the feet of the Royal Mail, it might be worth pointing out that Eliot only just sneaked into a 1995 set commemorating the 100th anniversary of the Nobel Prizes. The 45p stamp represents the prize for literature and contains 32 lines of Eliot's verse printed so small as to be illegible to the naked eye. Presumably the Royal Mail was drawing attention to the advent of nanotechnology at the same time.

Talking of the Nobel Prize, 2007 sees the centenary of Rudyard Kipling receiving his award for literature. He was the first English-speaker to win a Nobel and to this day remains the youngest (he was 32). This feat was recognised by Sweden way back in 1967, when a stamp was issued in Kipling's honour as part of the nation's celebrations of the 60th anniversary of the inauguration of the prize. In Britain we are too busy cashing in on Harry Potter to cast so much as a nod in the direction of Kipling, once described by Henry James as 'the most complete man of genius'.

The 21st century has, until the recent inclusion of Ian Fleming, seen a dearth of literary references in British stamps. Predictably the 50th anniversary of the publication of J.R.R. Tolkien's *The Lord of the Rings* was marked in 2004 with a special issue of a set of 'illustrations rarely reproduced or seen by the public'. Since I've seen many of these images in exhibitions at both the Ashmolean Museum and the Bodleian Library in Oxford, I can only assume this statement by the Royal Mail was an attempt to establish literary integrity for a set that was unashamedly riding on the coat tails of Peter Jackson's movie *The Return of the King* that had been released the year before and was storming the DVD chart at the time. Cynical maybe, but where there's hobbits, there's brass.

Another exception was in January 2006 when Peggy Fortnum's wonderful 1959 illustration of Paddington Bear made our morning post 'first class' in every sense. This was part of a set of 'Animal Tales' commems that included Beatrix Potter's Jeremy Fisher (who first appeared in 1905) as well as Helen Oxenby's White Rabbit from *Alice's Adventures in*

Wonderland (interestingly, Lewis Carroll has always done well on stamps). In a Blairesque attempt to appear cool, the Royal Mail introduced the stamp depicting Roald Dahl's Enormous Crocodile as by the grandfather of 'Sophie Dahl, now a famous supermodel'. Not a whiff of Kipling's *Jungle Book*, of course.

A big and rather sheepish thank you to the readers who wrote to me to describe an exquisite set of Kipling commems that had been released by the Post Office to universal critical acclaim. I must have missed them.

CHAPTER 8

O, what a phoney anniversary

ANOTHER ANNIVERSARY of a key moment of the Great War. Keen observers will note that maybe I'm a little early in publishing my column on the subject, but by the time November comes we'll all be suffering from First World War fatigue. We'll have had our fill of Tommy Atkins in the trenches, the mud and the blood and, of course, as Commander Flashheart so eloquently put it in *Blackadder Goes Forth*, 'all that *bloody* poetry'.

There's a very strong sense in which I was born to write this, if only because I came into this world on 11th November in a year when that date fell on a Sunday. The day being both the Anniversary of the signing of the Armistice and Remembrance Sunday, I'm lucky not to have been christened 'Poppy'. Perhaps it's because of this calendarial happpenstance that the Great War has always held me in its macabre, ghoulish and futile grip. What interests me most is how the industrial-scale slaughter has modulated into poetic acceptability. While we all love the myths of moonlit football matches in no-man's land, for decades no one really wanted to know about the mock crucifixions, the execution of shell-shocked deserters and the ritualised abuse of conscientious objectors. When the awful reality of the experience of the men on the Front Line became public property in the poetry of Wilfred Owen, it was quickly brushed under the carpet, with W.B. Yeats dismissing his work as 'blood, dirt and sucked sugar-stick'.

Even the moment we commonly perceive to be the conflict's end has a numerological poetry to it: the eleventh hour of the eleventh day of the eleventh month. We think of it finishing with the stroke of a pen in a railway carriage deep in the forest of Rethondes near the sleepy French town of Compiègne. The signatures brought into effect no more than a ceasefire that, due to inefficient communications along the Western Front, went largely unobserved. Despite this established fact, tradition still has it that the last man to die was Private George Price (Regimental Number 256265); shot that day by a German sniper at 10:58am. The Hun playing to the whistle again...

The history books tell us this was not the end: a formal state of war between the Allies and the Central powers persisted for another seven months until the Treaty of Versailles was signed on 28th June 1919, which explains why so many village war memorials commemorate 'the Great War 1914-19'. But even this wasn't technically the end of the war. The final act came about in 1923 when the Allies signed a peace treaty with what was to become the Republic of Turkey.

53

While both the small and silver screens relentlessly bombard us with visual glorifications of the heroism and romance of the Great War, the current fashion in the world of books is to let the figures do the talking. This trend was led in part by one of the best analysts of the topic – Niall Ferguson – in his *The Pity of War*. A work of economic political history, it examines the national budgets of the Entente and Central powers, with Ferguson concluding that, just as the colossal increase in global expenditure on arms made the outbreak of war inevitable, the equally predictable collapse of the protagonists' economies meant that neither side could sustain its participation. By mid-1918 it was fiscal *narpoo* all round, rendering the notion of who had 'won' largely academic. Understandably, Ferguson's icily detached book didn't please everyone.

A quick look around the bookshop at the Imperial War Museum in Lambeth confirms that most of the literature of the Great War relates to individual campaigns, military analysis, social and economic history and biographies of generals. However, there is an increasing body of more personal literature finding its way into print as the younger generations turn out their attics and publish collections of letters, diaries and memoirs of the ordinary soldier. Oral historians have been frantically travelling the length and breadth of the land to record the final thoughts of the last of the Great War veterans, who are now exclusively centen-arians. Maybe it's a sign of the times, but you can read Private Harry Lamin's 'blog' online, made up of transcripts of his letters from the front, posted on an ongoing basis exactly 90 years after he wrote them.

Of the personal recollections there's no more revealing book about the war than I.M. Parsons' classic anthology of contemporary poetry *Men Who March Away* (1965). Despite it being required reading for English undergraduates at Oxford during the 1980s it's still a favourite of mine, I suspect due to Parsons' gritty refusal to romanticise the war. His opening section – 'Visions of Glory' – is astonishing in that we find that some of the war's severest critics started out inspired by its poetic possibilities. There are pro-war poems by Edward Thomas, Isaac Rosenberg, Siegfried Sassoon and Thomas Hardy, whose 'Song of the Soldiers' gives the title to the anthology. In later life Sassoon claimed that his bloodthirsty *The Kiss* was an 'exercise in Anglo-Saxon words' (whatever that means). In truth, it's extraordinarily and gratuitously violent, without a trace of satire, and it is easy to see why he came to regret writing it.

As with many good anthologies, there are notable (and I suspect in Parsons' case, deliberately provocative) absences, the most obvious being that of Lt Col John McCrae's *In Flanders Fields*, written in 1915 during the Second Ypres. Some of the so-called 'remembrance tourism' operators will take you to the exact spot where the poem was written. It's now a small immaculate Commonwealth War Graves Commission cemetery by the side of a quiet country road where perhaps a few hundred British soldiers are buried. Middle-aged men and women accompany weeping parents to lay fresh flowers at row after row of identical Portland limestone graves. This was where I discovered that the headstones that are erected with no space between them mark the burial place of men who died together, whose body parts could not be separated. I went there in 2004 on my way to the Menin Gate to hear the Last Post at sunset as part of the commemorations of the 90th anniversary of the start of the Great War. It's easy to be cynical about all these anniversaries but, as these defining moments in modern history begin their progression from living memory to the dusty confines of the archive, perhaps we should be grateful for the recollections of the ordinary soldiers as well as the professional poets.

CHAPTER 9

Cash in a Flash
on the high street

O N THE 2nd January 2008 the *Daily Telegraph* announced on its front page the death of George MacDonald Fraser. The following day, in an affectionate obituary of the length normally reserved for statesman, the same newspaper was to describe the author's historical fiction as 'richly comic'. There's not much I can add, other than to say that, when the history of the 20th-century novel is written, it is my sincere hope that Mac-Donald Fraser's adopted character Harry Flashman will be entered into the canon as one of the great icons of military literature, to rank alongside Patrick O'Brian's Jack Aubrey or C.S. Forester's Horatio Hornblower.

Brigadier-General Sir Harry Paget Flashman VC, KCB, KCIE: Chevalier, Legion of Honour; Order of Maria Theresa, Austria; Order of the Elephant, Denmark (temporary); US Medal of Honor; San Serafino Order of Purity and Truth, 4th Class, was one of the great scoundrels of modern literature, and was, as the *Telegraph* so correctly adduced, 'the cad to end all cads'. In a way it was fitting that the character was pinched from Thomas Hughes's *Tom Brown's Schooldays*, and for many of his legions of fans it was a matter of mixed sentiment that, as the *roman-fleuve* progressed to its dozenth volume, Flashy started to find a moral centre and develop something akin to a conscience. He may have got off to a shaky start, and his early character may be hard to reconcile with the more mature bounder who roars and rogers his way into our affections, but Flashman stands for something; and, hard as it may be to believe, he stands as a symbol of decency. The trick with Flashman, and MacDonald Fraser knew it only too well, was that you can get away with any amount of cowardice, fornication and poltroonery provided you are not *entirely* bad to the bone. George MacDonald Fraser was an upright and honourable man – and you won't find anyone prepared to say anything different – but he didn't have much time for fashionable thinking or political correctness. Through his best-known character he found a voice to speak for those bored with the risk-averse, focus group, spin-ridden nanny state. And this is why we like him.

Not quite so honourable and upright is the e-mail I received on 6th January from Hatchards, the High Street book vendor that styles itself on its ostentatiously British corporate livery as the 'oldest and best bookshop in London'. The correspondence starts by alerting its e-mail customer database to the fact that MacDonald Fraser has died, before sighing that he 'would come and sign all his new books at Hatchards and we were proud to host a signing session with him in October of last year for his novel, *The Reavers*.' At this point I started to sense vultures circling and so wasn't particularly surprised by the following sentence: 'You might be interested to know that we still have signed copies of this book in stock in the following editions...' These editions being the standard hardback, which sells for £18.99, or a 'signed, numbered and slip-cased hardback, limited to 1,000 copies, £35'. The latter is little more than a publisher-vendor marketing gimmick and has nothing to do with the world of collectable books (interestingly both 'editions' have the same ISBN, making the distinction between the two blurred to say the least). And yet, the e-mail implies that the limited edition is a better investment than the standard, because 'please note that the £18.99 hardbacks are not signed on the title-page, but have been instead signed by the author on a blank page in front of the title-page'. Which is, as we shall see, more than can be said for the limited ones.

Let's have a look. Well you can try, but you will fail because the product (it's not a book anymore) is sealed in polythene shrink-wrap. Nowhere on the packaging does it state what the limitation is, so I rather reluctantly disbursed £35 in order to examine the contents at my leisure. Having removed the shrink-wrap (and presumably halved its second-hand value in the process) I was astounded to find that all the punter gets for his money is an adulterated regular edition in a box (complete with dust-jacket stating the recommended retail price in the UK of £18.99). Even more alarming is that the page bearing the author signature and stating the limitation is not part of the book at all, being in fact a tipped-in sheet between the front endpaper and the title-page. The limitation I can confirm is 1,000 (my copy is No 653), but of course nowhere does it tell us that, since half of the books published in the UK sell fewer than 250 copies, the limitation is all but meaningless (especially as *The Reavers* isn't a Flashman novel and so doesn't have a ready-made market).

It's hard to articulate my contempt for such shoddy work by Hatchards, but I will try. To charge £35 for such garbage is downright highway robbery. To send out hard-sell e-mails explicitly capitalising on the death of this extraordinary giant of historical fiction is to insult his memory. And to slyly mislead the public regarding the value of the spurious 'limited edition' on offer is underhand. Of course, Hatchards will say that they are only offering what the market wants. Even so, it will be interesting to see if the market will take up the second-hand copies of *The Reavers* 'limited edition' that are already doing the rounds on the internet for over £100. Will they merely lurk in cyberspace, or actually end up in a collection somewhere?

The irony of course is that even the fantastically opportunist Flashman would have had nothing to do with such amateurish exploitation of the punter. The big difference here is, for all his countless faults, Flashy had class. What he would have done would have been to order the entire stock off the shelves and put them into storage in his attic. Not for reasons of public sensibility, you understand, but because in a few years' time you might, just might, make a few quid from flogging these copies of *The Reavers* without drawing attention to the crass consumerism behind the venture.

On the 5th January 2010 – almost two years to the day since their first marketing communication on the subject – I received another e-mail from Hatchards informing me that the Piccadilly bookseller was 'pleased to announce' that some of its 'Signed Special Editions' were now available at half price, 'while stocks last'. The list included George MacDonald Fraser's The Reavers, described semi-literately thus:

> Elizabethan England, and a dastardly Spanish plot to take over the throne is uncovered. It's up to Agent Archie Noble to save Queen and country in this saucy and swashbuckling romp from the bestselling author of 'The Flashman Papers' and 'The Pyrates'. Spoiled, arrogant, filthy rich, and breathtakingly beautiful, the young Lady Godiva Dacre is exiled from the court of Good Queen Bess (who can't abide red-haired competition) to her lonely estate in distant Cumberland, where she looks forward to bullying the peasantry and getting her own imperious way. Little does she guess that the turbulent Scottish border is the last place for an Elizabethan heiress, beset by ruthless reivers (many of them unshaven), blackmailing ruffians, fiendish Spanish plotters intent on regime change and turning Merrie England into a ghastly European Union province. And no one to rely on but her half-witted blonde school chum, a rugged English superman with a knack for disaster, and a dashing highwayman who looks like Errol Flynn but has a Glasgow accent.
>
> To say nothing of warlocks, impersonators, taxi-drivers riding brooms, burlesque artists, the drunkest man in Scotland, and several quite normal characters. This special edition is signed, numbered out of 1,000 and presented in a slipcase.

On offer at £17.50, this edition of The Reavers, having languished on the shelves for more than two years, had only been reduced in price by £1.49. Shameful.

CHAPTER 10

Lost library in Lambeth

C HOKED WITH traffic, Norwood Road is so
completely encased in concrete that in summer it
becomes Lambeth's equivalent of Death Valley.
Temperatures soar off the dial, sirens wail, and irritated
locals flee to the green oasis that is nearby Brockwell Park.
Just across the road from the park and up towards Tulse
Hill there is a different kind of oasis. Herbarium, scientific
garden and library, the South London Botanical Institute is
reassuringly out of step with the daily grind of the 21st
century metropolis. Its founder – Victorian Englishman
Allan Octavian Hume – couldn't have predicted the transformation that the then smart and leafy suburb of Tulse Hill
was to undergo.

Hume was a civil servant by trade, an ornithologist by
inclination, and a political reformer by instinct. One of the
great men of the Victorian era, his founding of the institute
warrants no more than a few paragraphs in the final
chapter of his biography, and yet it has allowed one of the
most charming and tiny libraries in London to flourish.

Hume spent much of his civil service career in British-governed India, and at one time was Commissioner of Inland Customs with responsibility for Empire's Customs Line on the sub-continent. The 'Line' was in fact a 14-foot-high cultivated barrier of spiny Indian plum and thorny acacia that ran from the top of the Punjab down through Rajasthan – otherwise known as the 'Great Hedge'. On his return to Britain in the new century, inspired by his developing interest in spiritualism and Buddhism, his life followed a series of twists that included entering radical politics and transferring his intellectual allegiance from ornithology to botany.

Edward C. Moulton, in his introduction to the re-issue of Sir William Wedderburn's 1913 biography of Hume (a first edition of which is on the open shelves in the institute's library), writes with a lightness of tone not normally associated with the Oxford University Press that botany 'unlike ornithology was not incompatible with his continuing commitment to the principles of vegetarianism'. Roy Moxham, in *The Great Hedge of India*, goes a little further. Commenting on Hume's diaries (held in the Natural History Museum, along with his collection of 63,000 birds and 15,500 eggs), Moxham says that they are 'a catalogue of slaughter. Some days dozens of birds were shot, often for just a single specimen.'

It is arguable that the jewel of the South London Botanical Institute is its herbarium. This is a noteworthy collection of 100,000 specimens of (mostly) flowering plants from the British Isles and Europe, of which Hume bequeathed some 40,000. But for me the best bit of any visit to the Institute is time spent in its library. Although parts of the collection are scattered all over this enormous house, the nucleus is in a gloriously antiquated bay-fronted room with Bakelite switches, linoleum flooring and dark brown wooden shutters.

The Institute's wardens, Helen and Alex, tell me that the library was based on Hume's own collection of botanical books, some of which are still on the open shelves ('although the really good stuff is kept in a special room upstairs'). Even so, one of the beauties of the library is that so much of it dates back to the Victorian era, for many the Golden Age of botanical collecting. Some important volumes have been rebound, some are falling apart – nigh on priceless botanical monographs share the same shelves as battered old 'New Naturalist' and *Dictionary of Gardening*-type workhorses. It is after all a *working* library – although, if you wish to visit, your botanical muse must have a good sense of time because the institute opens for a mere six hours per week, between 10am and 4pm on Thursdays, 'other times by appointment'.

Highlights include some immense works of scholarship, ranging from Fawcett and Rendell's *Flora of Jamaica* (including several volumes on dicotyledons alone) to the forbidding German-language *Flora von Mittel-Europa*. There is Alphonse and Casimie's *Monographiae Phanero-amarum*, Kunth's *Enumeratio Plantarum*, Lowe's *British and Exotic Ferns*, the slightly confusing Britten and Holland's *English Plant-Names*, a whole shelf of Darwin's lesser known works, including *Vegetable Mould and Earth-Worms*, and much more besides, including most of the known published biographical material on Hume himself. Apart from books, there are constant reminders that you are in a botanical library. The centrepiece of the main work surface (that looks old enough to have been Hume's dining table) is a sprig of rhododendron in a glass of water (to be precise, it is *Dauricum parviflorum* that, according to a hand-written note, 'flowers in mid January'). On cupboard 28, next to Hooker and Jackson's *Index Kewensis*, sits the cone of the Bhutan Pine (*Pinus wallichiana*), quarantined in a plastic bag with a warning to handle it with gloves. There is a cameo of Charles Linnaeus in a specimen box, a rotating calendar 'presented by C.P. Castell esq, 21st October 1948' and a diagram that shows six techniques for making traditional Hawaiian *lei* (or flower garlands). There is also a small collection of botanists' vasculums dating back to the mid-19th century. A sign describes how these collecting cases had a popular secondary function and were routinely used for 'accommodating another British invention, the sandwich'.

In a lecture room that doubles up as the 'stacks' (mostly academic journals and periodicals), there is a superb photograph of Hume sporting a splendid soup-strainer almost as mighty as the 'Great Hedge' itself. On the mantelpiece, under a glass dome, there is his original microscope, while an old-fashioned display case shows drawings from his expedition to Yarkand in China. A framed sheet of Indian postage stamps commemorating the great man serves as a reminder that his place in history has been assured not for his prowess as a collector of botanical and ornithological specimens, but as a champion of the common man in India. Hume will rightly be remembered, in the words of his first biographer Wedderburn, as the 'Father of the Indian National Congress'. This was the party Mahatma Gandhi would later lead to take India to independence, and a party that would subsequently rule independent India for years.

CHAPTER 11

The world
according to Zadie

T HE WORLD would be a sad place indeed if there
were no mavericks to stand up and shake their fist
at the establishment, but when novelist Zadie Smith
recently did so in an attack on the major literary prizes in
the UK she found herself attracting very little sympathy. The
broadsheets had a field day when Smith, recipient of two
coveted literary awards, dismissed competitions such as the
Man Booker as being 'only nominally' about literature. In
their rush to point out that Smith is currently the chair of
a panel of judges in a literary competition, the *Telegraph* and
the *Sunday Times* almost forgot to point out that Smith was
devaluing her own achievements while inviting the literary
world to award her no more. No, the hacks in Fleet Street
were too busy chortling over yet another faux pas from the
novelist, whose angst-ridden panel is so paralysed by its
literary ideals that it is unable to confer an award.

The fact that Smith has decided not to award a prize is

legitimate. To many, this may appear lofty, to some perhaps stupid, considering there were, it transpires, some well-respected authors among the contestants. But how the *Willesden Herald* chooses to run its short story competition is its own affair. In justifying her absolutist position, Smith makes an extraordinary sideswipe at the sponsors of, dare I say, the more established literary prizes. She writes that these internationally recognised awards are 'about brand consolidation for beer companies, phone companies, coffee companies and even frozen food companies'. She's too coy to name the sponsors, so I'll do it for her: Whitbread, Orange, Costa and Iceland (the food retailer behind the original Booker competition). While it's tempting to ask what she thought the sponsorships were intended for, if not brand consolidation, Man Booker spokesman Ion Trewin raises a more important point when he asks: 'Why has she been so happy to accept money from these prizes and sponsors, who she now attacks?'

Part of the reason may be the deep human psychological 'Law of the Prize' that states that those without prizes must crave them beyond all else, while those in receipt must at least feign indifference to them ('What, this old thing? I think it must have been my turn...') My interest in Smith's edict is her assertion that established literary prizes are 'only nominally' about literature (actually, they are nominally about the *sponsor*, but we'll let that pass). While Smith's comment may show a graceless lack of tact in an author who has scooped two of them – she got a Whitbread for *White Teeth* in 2000, and an Orange for *On Beauty* in 2006 – you could argue that she is at least in a position to know what she is being controversial about. The fact that she's made these comments *after* judging a literary competition speaks volumes and leaves me feeling some sympathy for the novelist's position. There was a time when I felt pretty much the same way as Smith.

It was summer 2004 when I was asked to be a judge on the Thomas Cook Travel Book Award. I had been invited to join a panel of writers and editors chaired by the distinguished historian and former Director of the Royal Geographical Society, John Hemming. Although a little daunted by the steadily increasing pile of books in my hallway, I decided that this was the ideal opportunity to bring myself up to date with contemporary travel writing. And so I squared my shoulders and read the whole lot, little knowing at the time that most of the 90 volumes that had passed before my eyes were destined for Oxfam on Streatham High Road. Now, I know that all judges *say* that most of the stuff they read was rubbish, but quite frankly hardly any of the 2004 crop was worth chopping trees for. There were however bright stars in an otherwise dull firmament and, after several boozy lunches at the Travellers (and one stupendous dinner at the Goring), we rather tentatively published our shortlist.

My biggest setback was that my favourite had already fallen at the first and hadn't made the shortlist, while my second favourite, although on the shortlist, wasn't going to win. I knew this because, with the panel split in all directions, a travel book set in Papua New Guinea would be filtered out because there were no olives in it. (Conventional wisdom in travel book publishing has it that, the higher the olive count, the more popular the book will be). Bowing to the inevitable, I ruefully cast my vote with the increasing majority who wanted the award to go to a perfectly competent travelogue set in North America. This sense of anticlimax was not diminished by the author sending his parents to collect his cheque at a ceremony that understandably never really got off the ground and petered out with a few of the judges repairing to the Samuel Pepys in Green Park. Nothing has been heard of the Thomas Cook Travel Book Award since and, while the world is definitely unhappier for its demise, its 25th and final instalment could hardly be accused of being a classic.

A few weeks after the ceremony I received a modest (and I mean modest) honorarium from the organiser. While waiting in a queue to deposit the cheque, it suddenly occurred to me that there had been nothing in the process of judging these 90 books that had advanced the cause of travel writing: I felt dully aware that I had been instrumental in making a compromise decision as to the overall winner; had been appalled by the dearth of literary talent on offer; and had helped a populist mass tourism brand to align itself with the quest for literary excellence.

All of which sounds curiously similar to Zadie Smith's recent pronouncement, which, if I have unpicked it correctly, seems to say: if there are no entries worthy of an award, don't award one; literary competitions are not about literature, while sponsors are only in it to promote their brand. My experience with the Thomas Cook Travel Book Award taught me that, while Smith's first point may have a flawless internal logic to it, you will provoke less controversy by applying to it more relativistic principles. Second, I'm afraid it is no great insight to say that in the real world (as opposed to the *Willesden Herald*) the desire to make a popular decision is stronger than the desire to make the right one. And finally, while we are probably all bored half to death with a continuous bombardment of marketing messages, I'm afraid it is only good manners to be grateful to any sponsor who, for whatever reason, wishes to patronise the arts.

I still can't work out if the above is an attack on or a defence of Zadie Smith, though I sincerely hope that she took it as the latter. The reason for this softening of approach is that since writing this I met her by pure chance. We were both browsing in Hatchards on Piccadilly and, recognising her, I abandoned nearly all dignity and introduced myself. She wasn't at all irritated and we chatted amiably for a minute or two, after which I abandoned what was left of my dignity and asked her to inscribe the copy of On Beauty *that was by now in my hands. She asked for my name and when I told her she looked up, smiled and told me it was her favourite name. I didn't like to ask, so I thanked her and went on my way. When I got home I looked her up on Wikipedia, where I discovered that her husband's name is Nick.*

CHAPTER 12

Anyone for
'coronation cricket'?

ONE OF THE good things about being a reviewer is that occasionally an unsolicited book of rare brilliance lands on the welcome mat. Although only once in a blue moon, these moments are nonetheless as beautiful, and never more so than the unexplained arrival of a newish edition of *English Cricket* by Neville Cardus, the great music and cricket writer on the *Manchester Guardian* (as the much diminished *Guardian* newspaper was called until 1959). Although I was puzzled by the arrival of this Prion edition (no press release, accompanying letter or publisher statement), the pleasure of seeing a reprint of this classic was sufficient to temporarily distract me from the mounting frustration of installing a new scanner.

This feeling of confusion was increased when I noticed that this edition wasn't the same size as the contemporary version I've got tucked away in a box of old scorecards somewhere in Smith Towers. Having said that, this was unquestionably Cardus's original text. And while the inside flap of the dust-wrapper proudly declares *English Cricket* to be of a series called 'Writers' Britain', this is in fact a repackaged volume from the much loved and collected 'Britain in Pictures'.

Britain in Pictures was originally published in the 1940s, presumably with the intention of lifting public morale that had been so affected by the inhumanity of the Second World War and the privations of economic destitution that followed. That the series was hardly luxurious was compensated for by Collins' ability to commission some of the literary big guns of the era, including John Betjeman, Edmund Blunden, Lord David Cecil, Edith Sitwell, Graham Greene and of course Neville Cardus. Although the series was called '*Britain* in Pictures' (my italics), many of the individual titles seem to express a deeper and more ancient patriotic sentiment: *English Villages*, *English Poets*, *English Country Houses* and *English Cricket*. Indeed, Greene's *British Dramatists* is something of a departure in that it is apparently the only volume in the Prion series of reprints to have the word 'British' in the title.

John Frederick Neville Cardus, who came from the 19th-century slums of industrial Manchester, wasn't just English. He was from the hard-drinking working-class England that fought two World Wars, hand-to-hand, shoulder-to-shoulder in the trenches and the shell holes of no-man's land. The illegitimate son of a 'genteel prostitute', he had no formal education to speak of and became a journalist simply by copying the style of journalists he admired in the *Manchester Guardian*. When the First World War broke out, unable to take part in active service due to myopia, he took advantage of the employment vacuum, adopted the name Neville and began signing his articles 'NC'. A generation later, at the outbreak of the next war and fearing he was about to lose his job, he migrated to Australia, where he ended up as the *Sydney Morning Herald*'s music critic. It was during this time, on the other side of the planet, that he wrote *English Cricket*.

Maybe it was his geographical separation from the game's spiritual home, or maybe it was his inability to play an active role in a war that would change everything, but in *English Cricket* Neville Cardus produced one of the most quintessentially English books. To read this nostalgic vignette is to hear the chock of leather on willow, the distant hum of Spitfires over the duck-egg blue pavilions of Canterbury, and the ripple of applause at stumps for another unbeaten Jack Hobbs century. Of course it's propaganda, though I suspect no one who loves cricket will mind for one moment being seduced by the unattainable ideal of the English gentleman at play.

If Cardus's brief was to evoke the spirit of pastoral Albion then he could not have done it any better. His rhetoric is that of a radio script and there is music in every beautifully turned sentence. 'We might conjecture without too much fancifulness,' writes Cardus, 'that the advent of the fast "round-arm" attack hastened the passing of the tall hat which superseded the pretty three-cornered hat worn at Hambledon when the game was called "elegant and manly".' Of C.B. Fry's Herculean 232 not out at Lord's in 1903 Cardus is in his pomp: 'Never since has such batsmanship been seen as this for opulence and prerogative; it was symbolical of the age's prestige. It occurred a year after the Coronation of Edward VII; and it was indeed Coronation cricket, yet one more swaggering pageant reaching to a glittering horizon… And Fry, the Sir Willoughby Patterne of the batting crease, handsome and absorbed in himself, not playing the bowling but using it entirely for some private pleasure, a connoisseur in the dialectic of batting.' Only Cardus could allude to the hero of Meredith's *The Egoist* in a description of what is, according to some sources, only a game.

None of this will come as a shock to those aware of Cardus's other calling, that of music critic (for those keeping score, Cardus wrote 11 books on music and nine on cricket). Everyone knows that the combination of cricket and music critic is incontestably the best job in the world, and so to be knighted for the privilege borders on over-indulgence. This was not lost on the great all-rounder, who once said that to be paid to watch cricket at Lord's in the afternoon and then to hear Lotte Lehmann as Strauss's Marschallin in the evening 'was nothing less than an act of Providence'.

That the sport of cricket has produced such an extraordinary writer should hold no surprises. After all, cricket attracts the articulate, the artistic and the statesmanlike. No other sport has produced a John Arlott or a Brian Johnston; a Mike Brearley, a John Major or a Scyld Berry. And with the excellence of the current generation of cricket writers and broadcasters that includes journalists of the stature of Christopher Martin-Jenkins, Jonathan Agnew and Derek Pringle, we can be sure that the tradition Cardus did so much to enrich will be safeguarded for generations to come.

CHAPTER 13

Enchantress
and the lack of magic

REGULAR READERS of *Double Booked* will know that
I've never been a great admirer of Hatchards, who
seem to be prepared to do just about anything to
make money. Perhaps you shouldn't knock a business for
coming up with new ways of generating cash – we live, after
all, in what's supposed to be a free market economy, and just
because Hatchards are selling books doesn't necessarily
mean that they should behave in more gentlemanly a way
than, say, the music retail industry. But there are times when
I'm flabbergasted by the tawdry lows to which they are
prepared to sink.

Every now and then the Piccadilly bookseller dispatches
an e-mail alert announcing another signed limited edition
they're trying to offload onto the unsuspecting public. But,
it turns out, not all their e-mails are a complete waste of
time. I was very pleased they had been courteous enough to
notify me that Salman Rushdie was coming to Town to sign

copies of his latest, *The Enchantress of Florence*. I quite like Rushdie's books (despite him being very rude to me once at a party), and was especially keen to get him to sign my first edition of *The Satanic Verses* (1988).

It doesn't seem like twenty years ago. I can just about remember picking up my copy in an independent bookseller in Swansea, little knowing that it was to become one of the more important books of the decade (if not for its literary content, then for its potency as a misplaced symbol of Islamophobia). Of course, a first edition of *The Satanic Verses* isn't worth much. There are simply too many of them. Even a good one signed by the author is probably worth no more than £100. Much more important from the collector's viewpoint is *Midnight's Children* (1981), which can go for about five times as much. This is not on account of its Booker Prize success, but more for the failure of its predecessor *Grimus* (1975), the poor sales of which led Jonathan Cape to limit the first edition of *Midnight's Children* to about a thousand.

But I digress. Hotfoot to Hatchards where a posse of press photographers waiting in the street lent a certain atmosphere to the proceedings. Having bought my copy of the *Enchantress* I joined a queue of mostly middle-aged American ladies who seemed genuinely excited at the prospect of meeting their literary heart-throb (the guy's been married four times – he must have something...) Not so excited were the more serious collectors with carpet bags stuffed with every conceivable edition in the Rushdie *oeuvre*. These grim-faced aficionados were reacting predictably to the rumour that Hatchards had capped the number of books for signature at two per person. The absurdity of this petty bureaucracy was amplified by a rather prissy Hatchards official marching up and down the line demanding that anyone requiring a dedication by Rushdie should write it out on a piece of paper, as there was 'no time to waste explaining spellings'.

As I waited in the queue mildly completing the *Telegraph* crossword, I observed a surreal spectacle. The serious collectors were by now trying to buck the 'two-book rule' by soliciting others in the queue unencumbered by additional volumes to take their copies of *Fury* and *The Ground Beneath Her Feet* up to the great man for them. Maybe this is not such a daft idea, but it reminded me of when, as a student, I used to badger non-smokers to bring extra cigarettes through customs for me. It was all a little undignified and I couldn't but wonder why Rushdie was so disinclined to sign his own books for loyal fans who had crossed his palm with silver on many occasions.

It turned out that that he wasn't. When I reached the head of the queue I asked him if he minded signing my copy of *The Satanic Verses*. 'Not at all,' he said, before explaining that his ease with the situation derived from the fact that he had written it. 'I just don't feel so comfortable signing books I didn't write,' he elaborated, and off I went more than a little surprised by how charming he'd been.

If Rushdie was apparently happy to sign copies of his previous works, why should Hatchards object? The short answer is money. The way these things work is that the author isn't there for long, and to extract every last pound of flesh the bookseller needs to process the punters as quickly as possible. So you buy your book, form a queue, open the book to the title-page (not forgetting to write down your name in case the leading literary figure in attendance can't spell it) and prepare to be ushered through at the speed of an American doing Paris.

Which is all good for Hatchards' coffers, but not much of an experience for the collectors who have waited patiently to meet one of the most famous novelists on the planet. I'm only guessing, but I suspect most of these people would have liked to have shaken Rushdie's hand or posed for a photo with him; perhaps shared a brief anecdote, so that in years to come they could preface a sentence with, 'When I met Salman Rushdie...' But Hatchards being Hatchards this was a soulless affair, and I can only hope that Rushdie was paid handsomely for his appearance, because otherwise it would have been a complete waste of time for all concerned.

Of course this wasn't the first time I'd met Rushdie. On the other occasion he was neither polite nor charming. It was at the Polish Club on Exhibition Road, where Penguin was launching Ryszard Kapuściński's *The Shadow of the Sun*. The place was packed to the rafters with the literary great and good. Rushdie was with an exotic-looking Indian lady and a couple of moronic-looking minders. As it was an informal party I introduced myself as a magazine editor, and asked if he'd be kind enough to give me an interview. His prompt reply was in a vocabulary not usually associated with a publication as refined as *Bookdealer*. I'd expected him to say no, but I hadn't expected him to be rude.

But then again, maybe you're entitled to a little brusqueness when you've got a *fatwa* to contend with. Perhaps it was a condition of his recent knighthood that he brush up on his public relations, because at his recent signing of his *Enchantress* he was sweetness and light.

CHAPTER 14

Under Eastern eyes

T HERE ARE MANY theories as to why George Orwell
called his London novel *Nineteen Eighty-Four*. By
far the most plausible is that, sitting at his mechan-
ical typewriter in the year 1948, he simply switched the last
two digits. Although only a few decades in the future, to a
man who'd lived through the Second World War and whose
health was deteriorating, 1984 must have seemed a lifetime
away.

Nineteen Eighty-Four was in fact published in 1949, and
while this might appear to keen arithmeticians to be 59
years ago, the literary world has already started to celebrate
the 60th anniversary of the classic novel. I know this
because I have already started to receive requests to write
articles commemorating Orwell's masterpiece. In the course
of my research I met the multi-lingual Ukrainian-born
travel writer and novelist Vitali Vitaliev. A product of the
Soviet system, Vitaliev lived in the USSR under the Communist regime until his defection to the West in the early
1990s.

As we talked about Orwell it became clear that the literary freedom traditionally enjoyed in Western Europe is a source of some envy to those who have lived under totalitarian oppression. I naively assumed that anyone could read *Nineteen Eighty-Four* and was taken aback when Vitaliev told me that in the Soviet Union the punishment for being caught with a copy would almost certainly be a stretch in prison. And he readily confirmed for me that the word 'prison' in Russia means something considerably more daunting than it does here in the UK.

Vitaliev first read *Nineteen Eighty-Four* in Moscow in the late 1980s. He remembers a 'dog-eared paperback lent to me for one night only – the next morning I was to pass it on to the next person in line.' He stayed up all night reading and as dawn broke he remembers being moved almost to tears: 'How could someone who had never been to the Soviet Union, who had never lived under a totalitarian state, describe our lives with such poignant precision?'

When he first held the book, Vitaliev's 'hands shook'. It's hard to imagine a literary object having that much power (although according to her husband Leonard, Virginia Woolf's 'hands shook' as she typeset T.S. Eliot's *The Waste Land*). I've been to countries with non-democratic governments: in China I bought 'The Quotations from Chairman Mao Zedong' (otherwise known as *The Little Red Book*), and on one of my recent trips to Libya I got hold of Colonel Muammar al-Gaddafi's work of political philosophy, affectionately although unofficially dubbed *The Little Green Book*. But these seem almost like propagandist curios, or even ephemera. No, the business of Orwell in Russia was serious stuff. In the late 1980s a publisher caused a huge scandal in Moscow by daring to exhibit a copy of *Nineteen Eighty-Four* at the International Book Fair. Vitaliev, who was at the time working as an interpreter in the book trade, remembers an armed Soviet official screaming at the hapless publisher: 'You can exhibit anything – even Golda Meir if you wish – but not Orwell.'

The reason Orwell irritated the Soviet Central Committee was, of course, that he had got it all spot on. Stuff that I took to be graceful fiction was actually true. The Soviets rewrote the dictionary, adding hundreds of meaningless neologisms, just as Orwell had said. 'We had a real life Ministry of Truth,' said Vitaliev, 'only we called it the KGB. One of its departments was *Glavlit*, the state censorship agency.' The word *Glavlit* is a classic item of Newspeak derived from *Glavnoye Upravleniye Literaturi* (or 'Chief Directorate of Literature'). Nothing was safe from these censors: encyclopedia were edited post-publication, even after they had made their way onto private bookshelves.

One of the finest examples of this communist bowdlerization concerned the 'Beria affair', a story Vitaliev originally learned from his mother. In the early 1950s the head of the Soviet police and one of Stalin's henchmen, Lavrentiy Beria, had been exposed as a 'British Spy', and he was executed by firing squad in December 1953. The problem for the Party was that he still existed in every copy of the *Great Soviet Encyclopedia*. So *Glavlit* dispatched to every subscriber new pages for volume 'B' to replace the entry for Beria. Owners of the encyclopedia were ordered to paste the hopelessly overlong new article on the Bering Strait into position, literally papering over the past. *Glavlit* inspectors made random house checks to satisfy themselves that the instructions had been carried out to the letter. In *Nineteen Eighty-Four* the justification for altering historical texts is explained by the political philosophy that reality is what the Party says it is. In other words: 'He who controls the present, controls the past. He who controls the past, controls the future.' There are times when Orwell's Ingsoc ('English Socialism') and Soviet ideology bear more than a passing resemblance.

You don't see many first editions of *Nineteen Eighty-Four* these days, although at a recent book fair in Bloomsbury I saw a battered old thing that had been rebound in handsome black leather going for £450. Remembering Vitaliev's experience in Moscow I scanned around for armed Soviet officials, but there were none; just a few antiquarian book dealers eating their sandwiches and having a stab at the *Telegraph* crossword.

This special edition did, however, bring to mind something else Vitaliev had told me about a curious Russian edition of *Nineteen Eighty-Four*. 'Amazingly, those who controlled the printed word found it quite proper to read the banned books themselves,' said Vitaliev (after all, as Orwell said, some animals 'are more equal than others'). Soviet officialdom had developed a habit of producing limited editions of proscribed texts for consumption by the party elite. (This may remind you of Orwell's character O'Brien, who, as an inner party member, had a perfectly legitimate version of the banned *Theory and Practice of Oligarchical Collectivism* by Emmanuel Goldstein.) Vitaliev recalled how a friend's mother-in-law, who worked in the CPSU Central Committee library, saw such an edition of *Nineteen Eighty-Four* 'translated into impeccable Russian'. For anyone looking to get hold of a copy, it has a plain white cover with the number '59' and the word *Sekretno* ('classified') stamped on it. You couldn't make this stuff up, and it seems that George Orwell didn't have to.

CHAPTER 15

The truth about travel writing?

GERALD DURRELL'S *Golden Bats and Pink Pigeons* was one of my favourite childhood books, so rereading it on a flight to Mauritius, crisp chilled Chianti close at hand, was the fulfilment of an adolescent dream. I'd managed to get myself on an assignment to photograph the endangered wildlife of the Mascarene Islands, which includes the pigeon of Durrell's title. A quarter of a century ago this was one of the rarest birds on the planet, but today – thanks to Durrell's pioneering conservation techniques – there are more than 400 of them. And they're doing so well, they've been taken off the 'critically endangered' list.

I'd hoped to embark on an arduous and complex research programme prior to my departure, but by the time I'd got my logistics sorted I'd run out of time. All I really knew about the island most famous for being the home of the dodo was what the late Jersey zookeeper had written back in the 1970s. As the aeroplane began its descent over the Indian Ocean, I was just starting to enjoy the paradox of landing by plane on the land of the flightless bird, when Durrell made the same observation. And as I caught sight through the porthole of some of the most extraordinary volcanic topography, so did Durrell, and to my surprise it really did look like the molten lava had been churned 'as a chef whips egg whites until they become stiff and form weird peaks when lifted up on a fork tip'. Within a week we were climbing these mosquito-infested mountains, soaked to the skin and deafened by operatic thunderstorms. I wasn't so much recreating his journeys in pursuit of these endangered species as tagging along behind him.

All the while I was absolutely astounded by the accuracy of his writing. Millions of people have read Durrell's popular wildlife books, and since only a tiny percentage of them has ever had the opportunity to retrace his steps – in Cameroon, Guyana, Sierra Leone and the Mascarene Islands – the author had put himself in a position of trust. And if *Golden Bats and Pink Pigeons* is anything to go by, he was a reliable recorder indeed.

Travel writing hasn't always enjoyed such a close relationship with the truth. In the early days, there was absolutely nothing to stop you making it up as you went along. If you were a budding Ibn Battuta or an emerging Marco Polo, you could dress up your travelogue with any amount of serpents, grass-skirted pigmies, vampire bats and cannibals. Accuracy wasn't an issue, because there was no way of verifying anything you wrote. The less scrupulous of the early writers exploited this literary loophole, admittedly under pressure from their publishers, who rarely saw the point of allowing the truth to get in the way of a good story. Mungo Park's *Travels in the Interior Districts of Africa* (1816) is almost certainly sensationalised, although what the Scottish explorer got up to was nothing compared with John Keane, whose *Six Months in the Hijaz (1877-1878)* still causes controversy today. Keane's claim that he had met with an Englishwoman in Mecca caused such outrage back in England that the scandal was eventually debated in Parliament.

Keane's further claim that the woman had married a Muslim and did not want to be rescued somewhat back-fired, as the inquiry reportedly concluded that either Keane or the woman was insane and there was therefore nothing to be done. Keane milked his notoriety for all it was worth, and as a result of his PR endeavours his *Six Months* is still in print today. For sheer improbability, however, nothing beats Thomas Nashe's *The Unfortunate Traveller* (1594), whose protagonist Jack Wilton describes his progress through France and Italy engaged as a page to the Earl of Surrey. During his peregrinations he witnessed plague, rape, human dissection, ritual execution and devil worship. Nashe, who is perhaps most famous for coining more neologisms than Shakespeare, was clearly no stranger to fabrication.

None of this was lost on C.S. Lewis, who parodied such embroidery in his brilliant *Voyage of the Dawn Treader* (1952), whose episodic journey takes its crew to the lands of monopods, a fire-breathing dragon and a good old-fashioned slave market (that bears an uncanny resemblance to a description in *Zanzibar in Contemporary Times* by Robert Nunez Lyne FRGS, 1905).

Early cartographers were up to similar tricks. Don't know what happens on this blank space on the map? A three-headed serpent or a range of fictional mountains should fill it up nicely. This was not without repercussion: in the mid 18th-century the somewhat hapless Scottish explorer John Duncan, otherwise known as 'the King's stranger', embarked on an expedition to Dahomey in West Africa in order to pinpoint the exact location of the legendary Kong Mountains. Unfortunately for Duncan they were a work of the cartographic imagination and, having failed in his venture, he missed out on a lucrative sequel to his *Travels in Western Africa* (1846) – which I would have called *King Kong* – and died an understandably broken man.

None of this was of anything more than passing interest to Durrell, who claimed that he wrote simply to raise money for his wildlife conservation projects. He therefore had a vested interest in representing his animal-collecting expeditions as accurately as possible. To be exposed as anything other than a model of integrity and accuracy would have been catastrophic for his career. Despite writing one of the classics of 20th-century travel – *My Family and Other Animals* (1956) – he claimed to have no special love of writing, and cared even less for leaving his mark on posterity. This honour he would leave to 'brother Larry', who, as Lawrence Durrell, achieved fame as a poet and greatness as a novelist – although, if my sources are to be believed, he was a complete duffer at catching animals.

After this column was published I received a letter from the equestrian travel writer and explorer CuChullaine O'Reilly pointing out the serious omission of Daniel Defoe, who is supposed to have written his travelogues without ever leaving his desk. I wrote back to O'Reilly – who is the author of the blood-curdlingly superb Khyber Knights *– claiming to have deliberately left out Defoe in order to concentrate an entire article on him at a later date. I then promptly forgot.*

O'Reilly and his wife Basha are proprietors of the Long Riders Guild Press in the United States that owns the Classic Travel Book imprint. It was under this banner that John Duncan's Travels in Western Africa *finally made it back into print after being unavailable for more than a century. At the same time O'Reilly published the first biography of 'Scotland's forgotten explorer', who had been overshadowed by the titans of African exploration that followed him, notably David Livingstone, Richard Burton and Henry Morton Stanley. Called* The King's Stranger *this fascinating account of early exploration of the Dark Continent was written by amateur historian Derek O'Connor with a foreword by Robin Hanbury-Tenison.*

CHAPTER 16

Exploration
on the menu

THE LIBRARY of the Travellers Club in Pall Mall is probably the most beautiful of its type in the metropolis. I've been lucky enough to visit several times, usually attending book launches by some of the world's most famous explorers and travel writers. Robin Hanbury-Tenison celebrated the publication of the second edition of his seminal *Oxford Book of Exploration* there a few years ago and, more recently, Colin Thubron launched his *Shadows of the Silk Road* at the Travellers.

But there cannot have been many occasions to match a recent dinner I attended to celebrate the founding of the Cordon Rouge Club, a new society that has been set up to 'reward exceptional people for their extraordinary achievements within the realms of exploration, sailing, adventure and discovery'. A thoroughly modern explorers club in other words, although, as we shall see, with roots reaching deep into the Heroic Age of Antarctic exploration. It was also an occasion that inadvertently produced a superb piece of ephemera that will without a shadow of a doubt become a much sought-after item for any serious collector specialising in 21st-century exploration.

The full name of the club is the Champagne G.H. Mumm Cordon Rouge Club, which is of course derived from a particular brand of fizz with a diagonal red ribbon in its famous insignia. But it is also named after the man behind the champagne – Georges Hermann Mumm – who in the mid-19th century took the family business by the scruff of the neck and propelled his wine into the limelight with some pioneering corporate branding. It wasn't long before the international elite fell under his spell and G.H. Mumm Champagne became known as 'The Champagne of Kings'.

Georges Mumm was a fanatical traveller who numbered among his friends the intrepid Captain Jean-Baptiste Charcot. A leading explorer of his day, Charcot was the French equivalent to Scott or Shackleton and the first Frenchman to set foot on the continent of Antarctica. In 1903 Charcot set sail in a new-built 150-foot ship made entirely of oak, with a plan to gather botanical, zoological and meteorological data from the Antarctic waters. After encountering storms and icebergs, he decided to winter off the coast of Booth Island. The story goes that, in order to stave off boredom, in May 1904 Charcot organised a picnic on the ice for his crew. History has not left us with details of what his men ate, but we do know that Charcot's picnic was sluiced down with bottles of champagne that had been supplied to the expedition by his good friend Georges.

There is even a photograph of the event, where an immaculately dressed Charcot can be seen quaffing away while reading a newspaper and smoking his pipe. I'm not sure who delivered newspapers to Booth Island in those days, but then again I'm not sure the photo was even taken outdoors. The photograph's composition, lighting and sheer coziness has 'studio shot' written all over it.

The Cordon Rouge Club dinner was in many ways a reconstruction of this famous picnic, although guests at the Travellers without doubt experienced something altogether a little more flamboyant. The culinary highlight of the event was the 'champagne paired dinner'. I didn't have to wait long to find out what this curious expression signifies because it soon became obvious that it simply means you get a different champagne with each course. By the time the sumptuous Cuvee R Lalou 1998 that went with the roasted turbot with girolles had arrived I was getting the hang of it, and by the time the 'Rose jelly surrounding marinated red fruits' arrived I was pretty well marinated myself. The menu tells me that we sampled five different champagnes that evening (you of course have claret with the Welsh lamb and cognac with the coffee and truffles).

It was a memorable day. It will be hard to forget Club Chairman and all-round adventurer Bear Grylls decapitating a bottle of bubbly with a *sabrage* sword (this apparently dates back to the time of Napoleon, when his men developed the art of opening their champagne bottles without dismounting). But perhaps the most memorable part of the evening was the menu itself. G.H. Mumm do not do things by half, and so when the event organiser Charlotte Bell told me that the menu was going to be a collector's item I was intrigued to say the least. But nothing could have prepared me for the extraordinary hardback book that had been printed for the occasion. (The publishing of commemorative menus in book form dates back to the mid-19th century and there are examples of these in the library of the Royal Geographical Society, along with Sir Ernest Shackleton's famous sketch map of Antarctica that he drew on a menu.)

The menu produced for the first dinner of the Cordon Rouge Club is quite special: bound in brown cloth with gold tooling it also includes a red ribbon bookmark as a subtle homage to Georges Mumm's original branding (that in itself was a tribute to the Legion of Honour). The endpapers are a fascinating design based on Mumm's logo of crossed *sabrage* swords, a flowing ribbon and the initials 'CRC', while the body of the book itself is taken up with photographic portraits and potted biographies of the club members. It's beautifully designed, set in a reassuringly classy font (that might be Hoeffler) with some fascinating archive photographs from the Royal Geographical Society's collection that show how deep and long-lasting the relationship between exploration and champagne really is. There is a reproduction of the Midwinter Day Dinner from the *Terra Nova* British Antarctic Expedition 1910-13, with a relaxed Captain Scott at the head of the table; similarly, there is a photograph of the Midwinter dinner aboard *Endurance* from Shackleton's Imperial Trans-Antarctic Expedition 1914-17; there's a shot of Brigadier General Charles G. Bruce lubricating the tonsils, and there is Queen Victoria's birthday luncheon at Entebbe in 1900.

Realising the menu was something that would become a rare piece of ephemera, I abandoned all dignity and, between courses, circumnavigated the library badgering an increasingly convivial band of explorers for their autographs. My intention of course was to get the lot, but since polar balloonist David Hempleman-Adams had left for an early train I was immediately scuppered. Despite this setback, by the end of the evening polar explorers Tom Avery, Neil Laughton, Ben Saunders and Patrick Woodhead had all signed. Sir Robin Knox-Johnston, Bear Grylls, Ben Fogle, expedition artists Olly & Suzi all followed suit, along with just about every round-the-world yachtsman (and woman) that you could think of.

Naturally the idea caught on and before long eighty menus were flying around the Travellers Club library like bats in a cave. Despite Tom Avery's joke that they'd 'all be on eBay tomorrow', to the best of my knowledge not one has been sold yet and, in a funny sort of way, that's the way I hope it stays.

Prior to the event, guests had been reminded about the strict dress code of the Travellers Club that required gentlemen to wear 'jacket and tie, or national dress (no trainer shoes or denim) throughout the building ... Ladies are expected to dress to a similar standard.' Word went out that, while the evening wouldn't be 'black tie', gentlemen were required to wear lounge suits, while ladies may wear cocktail dresses. On the evening Bear Grylls turned up in a pink linen suit of several thousand decibels. As the evening wore on I found myself drawn into a drunken discussion on whether Mr Grylls considered himself to be wearing some sort of combination of lounge suit and cocktail dress. I was later told that he didn't find this at all funny, which was odd, because everyone else seemed to.

The second annual meeting of the Cordon Rouge Club was held at Rocklands Manor, Isle of Wight on 26th May 2009, where explorers Colonel John Blashford-Snell, Sir Chris Bonington, Sir Ranulph Fiennes, Rune Glendjes and Polly Murray were entered into the club membership. A menu similar to that of the 2008 dinner was produced to commemorate the occasion, only this time in red.

CHAPTER 17

Insects and vile ants

MAYBE I GOT off lightly, but I've only worked in a bookshop once in my lifetime, and that was way back in the mid-1980s when, on coming down from university, like so many English literature graduates before me, I decided to follow my star and join the book trade. It can't have been a very ambitious star because, if I may mix my metaphors, the apple didn't fall far from the tree. It merely plopped off the branch at Balliol College, rolled across Broad Street (neatly skirting a sunken cross marking the spot where the 16th-century Oxford martyrs Cranmer, Latimer and Ridley were executed) before ending its journey in the basement of Thornton's bookshop.

Thornton's had the staff of legend: Dickensian scriveners with pebble glasses toiling away at high clerks' desks by candlelight; intimidating multi-lingual eastern European women with encyclopaedic knowledge of every book ever published, and sour-faced academics with library tans resting for a few decades before returning to their doctoral theses. It was the sort of bookshop that wasn't really ready for the 19th century, let alone the 20th, and although Thornton's had been in business since 1835, by the early 1980s it was in terminal decline. It was eventually sold to Wim Meeuws of Holdan Books, and although I can't speak with absolute authority, it must have been a challenging time for the new proprietor. Only a few hundred yards down the road, Blackwell's was doing a roaring trade offloading new books onto freshmen clutching reading lists as long as their recently-acquired college scarves. Even at the age of 22, I could see that most of the stock Meeuws had inherited was tired, dilapidated and irrelevant to a busy university town. My guess is that the real money was made through the mail order business that went on behind the scenes, downstairs in the bowels of this labyrinthine Grade II listed building.

Meanwhile, old Mr Thornton (apparently known as 'young Jack') would sit in the shop day after day, scowling at anyone courageous enough to come in off the street and browse the stock. Occasionally someone interesting, such as Elizabeth Jennings or Isaiah Berlin, would come in, but for the most part Thornton's remained (on the surface at least) untroubled by anything that could be even remotely classified as 'eventful'. Yet beneath this veneer of antique respectability there was a whiff of poison in the air.

The shop assistants all seemed to be motivated by an irrational mistrust of each other. This is nothing new in the book trade, as John Saumarez Smith's *A Spy in the Bookshop* will testify. But there were times when this mistrust would boil over into downright hatred, a kind of intellectual germ warfare that made even the books on the shelves look depressed. Nearly every member of the cast was an eccentric of some sort, and by not being one I stuck out like a sore thumb. I was working simply to pay off the debts I'd accrued in my last year at college, and so when offered the job of order processing clerk I jumped at the chance. It was a poisoned chalice I knew, as hardly anyone stuck in the role for any length of time, and Thornton's wages were preposterously low even by book trade standards. And yet there was still the business of the star I was following, and so I bought myself a transistor radio (there was a 6-match Ashes series that year) and embraced the challenge.

As order processing clerk I served two functions. The first was to complete manual and pre-computerisation tasks, such as checking delivery notes, invoices and orders, unpacking boxes, preparing orders for the packer, going to the post office, and so on. The second was to arbitrate between the increasingly paranoid factions that were developing on the front line. Needless to say I was completely useless at both, and after a long hot summer of troglodytic dwelling in the cellar I cashed my last pay cheque and got the hell out of there. By way of reintegration into the real world I spent three days recruiting in the White Horse, where if I remember correctly I also celebrated a 3-1 series victory over Australia.

But life at Thornton's wasn't all bad. If nothing else, I learned a little about the inner workings of the book trade. The new proprietor was trying everything to make a success of the venture, including publishing a lovely facsimile reprint of Alfred Rimmer's rare 1878 *Pleasant Spots Around Oxford*. But of all the books that passed through my hands my favourite was another facsimile, this time of Vincent M. Holt's *Why Not Eat Insects?* Originally published in 1885, and reprinted by E.W. Classey of Faringdon in 1967 and at various intervals until 1978, its price in 1985 I can confirm was £1.50. I know this because I priced a batch of them myself in pencil on the front endpaper, before allowing one of them to fall into the pocket of my brown corduroy jacket.

I'm still not sure whether *Why Not Eat Insects?* is the work of a Victorian madman or visionary. His argument is basically that the poor are starving, and the biblically-endorsed eating of locusts, grasshoppers, crickets, snails, wasp grubs, sawflies, stag beetle larvae and so on make for good wholesome nourishment (before anyone writes in, I *know* not all of the above are insects – I am merely quoting some of the components in one of Vincent M. Holt's proposed menus). The author goes further, saying that these are the very blighters that destroy the agricultural crops planted to feed the rich. He continues by saying that the poor should be sent into the fields to harvest the offending fauna, and in so doing provide them not only with gainful employment, but also with the 19th-century equivalent of a Big Mac with Fries to go. 'I foresee a day,' says Holt, 'when the slug will be as popular in England as its luscious namesake the Trepang, or sea-slug, is in China, and a dish of grasshoppers fried in butter as much relished by the English peasant as a similarly treated dish of locusts is by an Arab or Hottentot.'

Why Not Eat Insects? was a unifying book at Thornton's. We all liked it, and it was something of a joke that, while the then popular D.M. Thomas was nothing but sex and violence, the worthy Vincent M. Holt was a far more edifying concoction of 'insects and vile ants'.

Today No 11 Broad Street is no longer a bookshop. Back in 2002 Wim Meeuws relocated his business to Boar's Hill, where he sells books via a mail order and internet company that keeps alive the name Thornton's. The historical building is now a café, where, if you are lucky enough to get a decent seat by the window and your imagination permits, you may over tea and scones contemplate the fate of the martyrs, roasted alive for refusing to recant their Anglicanism.

Believe it or not I received a letter from a reader stickling over my use of the word 'recruiting' where he felt I clearly meant 'recovering' or 'recuperating.' As a counter-stickle I refer my correspondent to The New Shorter Oxford English Dictionary *where the fifth definition of 'recruit' (admittedly tagged 'Now rare or obs.') reads in part 'renewal of strength or vigour'. I further refer him to Leonard Woolf's 'A Tale Told by Midnight' in* Stories of the East, *where the narrator correctly uses the word in its rare sense when he informs us, '... we were both staying with Alderton, the novelist. Mrs Alderton was away – recruiting after annual childbirth, I think.'*

CHAPTER 18

The perils
of polar printing

AS SAMUEL PEPYS might have noted: up betimes and we come to the National Maritime Museum in Greenwich, to a special exhibit of part of the Caird Library's collection of polar manuscripts, artefacts and printed books. Among the items on display: a wonderfully preserved copy of *Aurora Australis*, along with a decidedly rickety *The South Polar Times* bearing Rudyard Kipling's bookplate pasted onto the front endpaper. Both publications were of course edited by Sir Ernest Shackleton, the latter, according to Bonham's catalogue, one of the 'scarcest and most desirable books of polar literature, with copies selling for many thousands of pounds on the rare occasions when a set comes on the market'. For those of us who cannot wait for such a contingency, and who are prepared to unbuckle the purse to the tune of £600, there is always the Centenary Facsimile edition.

Published exactly a century ago in 1908, it is *Aurora* that fascinates me. It's intrinsically no more important than the *The South Polar Times*, but its romance lies in its being the first book to be printed and bound on the White Continent. I'm already on thin ice here, as Bernadette Hince's *Antarctic Dictionary* sternly disagrees with me, claiming that honour for the *Times*. The Royal Geographical Society's website describes the *Times* as the 'in-house magazine' of Captain Robert Scott's *Discovery* expedition, and while this may sound flippant it is an important reminder of the nature of the publication. While I accept the *Times* pre-dates Shackleton's *Nimrod* expedition during which *Aurora* was published at the 'Winter Quarters on the British Antarctic Expedition', I don't accept it is a printed book. I don't want to squabble with the *Antarctic Dictionary*, but Shackleton himself, in his Editor's Preface to *Aurora*, says that there were 'essential differences between the two efforts, for the South Polar Times was typewritten and only one copy could be issued, whereas Aurora Australis is actually printed, and therefore allows of a larger edition.'

This 'larger edition' has a different print run depending on who you talk to, but the most sensible estimates vary from a conservative fifty-five (quoted by the National Maritime Museum) to 'about a hundred', a number traditionally bandied about by prospective buyers looking to drive down the price. The explorer's only granddaughter, Alexandra Shackleton, tells me that the actual quantity of copies printed is probably somewhere in between: 'I think there were more than fifty-five.'

The story of how *Aurora* was printed is a tale of publishing derring-do that is strangely in keeping with spirit of the

Heroic Age of Polar exploration. In his 'Additional Preface' to *Aurora*, Sir Ernest writes: 'though I can see but little not up to usual standard in bookmaking, the printers are not satisfied that it is everything that it ought to be.' He goes on to explain that, due to the sub-zero temperatures in the hut where the printing took place, the only way to keep the ink in 'fit state to use' was to have a candle burning under the inking plate. The men responsible for the printing were petty officers Ernest Joyce and Frank Wild, who had taken a crash course in printing in London before heading south. They completed an apprenticeship that would normally occupy seven years in a mere three weeks at Sir J. Causton & Sons Ltd. who, not content with supplying the know-how, also kitted out *Nimrod* with 'an entire printing and lithographic outfit', including paper.

The Caird Library is named after Sir James Caird of Glenfarquhar, ship owner and benefactor of the National Maritime Museum. This particular James Caird should not be confused with another Sir James Caird, jute baron and philanthropist, who was the main sponsor of Sir Ernest Shackleton's Imperial Trans-Antarctic Expedition of 1914-16 (or *Endurance*, after the ship that sailed Shackleton and his men to the southern Polar Regions). This expedition has passed into legend, not because it succeeded in meeting its objective (Shackleton never got to the South Pole), but more for a Herculean rescue mission that has ensured Shackleton's place in history as one of the greatest ever leaders of men. Against all odds, 'the boss' successfully navigated 800 nautical miles in an open boat to South Georgia in order to relieve his crew, stranded on Elephant

Island after the loss of the *Endurance*. The 23-foot whaler that braved the bleakest of conditions was the *James Caird* (named after the philanthropist, not the ship owner). Returned to Britain in 1919, the *James Caird* now has a permanent home in the north cloister of Dulwich College (which also happens to be the home of the James Caird Society, which is dedicated to the preservation of Shackleton's memory). Prior to taking up residence at the college the plucky little whaler was kept at the National Maritime Museum, where there is now a life-size replica that was commissioned especially for the 2002 film *Shackleton*, starring Kenneth Branagh.

But I digress. The National Maritime Museum's copy of *Aurora Australis* is particularly interesting because it has been disbound for 'conservation reasons'. What this means is that it can be seen in its two component parts: the text block, which is as clean as a whistle, and the binding, which is made of plywood from recycled packing cases and spare harness leather. The plywood is actually a brand called Venesta, named after the London-based company that manufactured it, and clearly bears parts of the stenciled words 'British Antarctic'. Constructed by crewman and motor expert Bernard Day, the binding gives a fascinating insight into how the book was crudely stitched together, with three pairs of eyelets neatly drilled through the boards. A rather grand prelims page declares *Aurora* to have been:

> Printed at the sign of
> 'The Penguins'; by Joyce
> and Wild.
> Latitude 77° ·· 32′ South

Longitude 166° ·· 12′ East
Antarctica

About a dozen copies of *Aurora* have come up for sale since the turn of the century, all of them at auction. The most recent fetched £43,200 at Bonham's in 2007 (it had been fantastically described in the catalogue as the 'Black Tulip of any Antarctic collection'). This was by no means the most expensive, with one going in 2006 for £53,000. Compared with the decades leading up to the Millennium, today the market is awash. Despite this (or maybe even because of…?) it is unlikely, as one of my sources tells me, we'll see a copy go for 'less than US$100,000 again'. For the general reader it is perhaps as well that there is a print-on-demand edition of *Aurora Australis* available from the Classic Travel Book imprint of the Long Riders Guild Press, who will let you have a copy for under £20.

CHAPTER 19

More notes from
a Persian tea house

A NY JOURNEY of substance through Iran, or Persia as
you will end up calling this ancient country, takes
you to Yazd. As desert cities go, Yazd is about as
remote as it gets, and no matter from where you set off,
getting there is guaranteed to be a time-consuming affair.
As the narrow highways pick their course in between ferru-
ginous mountain ranges, the best thing to do is push on
while it is still light. On the Iranian Plateau, tall mountains
hem you in on all sides, and at night the salt-desert is a
curiously claustrophobic place.

The road from Shiraz to Yazd is long and dusty and, for
all the landscape's beauty, the miles blur into one. Pistachio
and walnut trees on the roadside start to become invisible,
and the occasional herd of pomegranate-chomping goats
only dimly registers. Soon you realise the desert is not the
place to get an annoying tune stuck in your head. Despite a
couple of nights at a *caravanserai* at the mid-point of the

adventure, there could no longer be any illusions as to the unremitting nature of the topography. Even the most positive traveller soon looks for a literary diversion. Within hours I discovered that one of the more frustrating ironies of travelling in Iran is that despite its name you'll never get a drop of Shiraz in its city of wine and roses. And so the evenings were spent polishing off Anthony Wynn's full-bodied *Persia in the Great Game* and Robert Byron's over-rated *The Road to Oxiana*. By the time I left for Yazd, all that was left of my travelling library was Michael Carroll's *From a Persian Tea House*, which I'd been avoiding. I'd never heard of the author, and since its publisher had recom-mended it as a 'forgotten gem of travel writing' I felt certain that it had been forgotten for a very good reason. But, after my disappointment with *Oxiana*, and having dispatched the last of my *Telegraph* crosswords with a regal flourish, in the Dasht-e Lut I felt that I had nothing to lose.

Carroll travelled through Iran in the 1950s, during one of the few periods of relative calm in Persia's busy and bloody history. As if taking on the character of the country at the time, this unexpectedly lovely travelogue weaves its meandering course through a country that had changed little since the dawn of civilisation. From the deserted ruins of Persepolis to the bustling tea houses of Esfahan, Carroll and I followed each other around Persia: he roughing it down dry river beds in his Land Rover, while I was bused along the tarmac behind tinted windows. Carroll was a good travelling companion and I liked his descriptions of old Persia, and in particular his wry vignettes of the tea house.

Taking tea in Persia is the most important thing in life and so not undertaken lightly. The tea house is equivalent to the Dog & Duck, where men meet to discuss matters of the day, to smoke apple-scented tobacco in water pipes or *ghalyan*, to discuss the price of oil or the forthcoming American presidential election. In Esfahan I drank tea several times with Hassan, who had been a shop assistant in London, a taxi driver in California and had fought in the Iran-Iraq war in the 1980s. He had now retired from a life of adventure and preferred to watch the world go by. 'I have seen many bad things,' Hassan told me as he put a trans-lucent disc of sugar onto his tongue. 'Now I prefer to drink tea and go to the Mosque.' In Yazd I had tea with a man whose shop seemed only to sell spinach.

Carroll reckoned that the Persian obsession with eating sugar is to blame for the nation's pre-Revolutionary addiction to opium. Decades of drinking tea sucked through sugar lumps had taken its toll on Persia's teeth. With no dental service to speak of, Persia's only solution to its collective toothache was to get smashed on opiates, and by chasing the dragon so chase away the pain. At one time there were two-and-a-half million addicts in the country all craving the poppy's oblivion. Carroll briefly mentions his own flirtations with opium before complaining that he never got the chance to try it in Persia. Much to his regret, all the opium dens had been shut down by the time he got there. On one night alone a thousand such places were closed in Tehran. Today, Iran takes a dim view of people smuggling heroin into Europe via the old Silk Road. Fed up with Westerners and their fancy digital cameras, at

Mehrabad airport a grumpy official searched my gadget bag for drugs. He removed the dust caps from my lenses, squinted down their barrels, covered the filters with fingerprints and said: 'Canon is no good. Use Nikon.'

From a Persian Tea House had enthralled me from the word go, and Carroll is never better than when describing his arrival at the Friday Mosque in Yazd. He'd been impressed by a photograph that Robert Byron had taken here in the 1930s (and subsequently published in early editions of *Oxiana*) and had decided to recreate it if he could. Enjoying the literary link between the two books I'd so recently read, I also decided to recreate the photograph. On my arrival I took stock of my surroundings, and immediately agreed with Carroll that Byron must have taken his picture from the rooftop of the bazaar to the left of the mosque's entrance.

In the blazing mid-afternoon sun, I strode up to the bazaar keeper with the easy air of a man with a clear conscience. As I speak no Farsi, and most Iranians in the remoter desert towns speak no English, I slipped effortlessly into the *lingua franca* of Persian travel. To some, this is a grotesque sequence of comic gestures, facial contortions and muted snorts. But they are wrong: it is in fact a graceful, fluid mode of discourse, and I was becoming very good at it.

'Salaam,' I started. It was a good start and I felt my work here was already half done. 'I am a writer from England,' I gestured and snorted. 'I would like to take a photograph of the mosque from the roof of your bazaar.' He obviously understood every word because within minutes he was propelling me gently by the elbow through the dark recesses of his shop. He guided me past towering piles of embroidered cushions, row upon row of *ghalyan*, turquoise and silver necklaces, boxes of saffron-flavoured crystal sugar, silk weavings, postcards and Persian carpets. At the back of the store a rough old *kilim* was slung over a washing line, forming a makeshift curtain concealing a padlocked metal door to a flight of rickety stairs. In the deep shade of the stairwell there was a scruffy marmalade tomcat choking on chicken bones, thin plastic bags full of charcoal and some decomposing pomegranates surrounded by wasps. I'm not coming with you, gestured the man who as an afterthought added, let me know when you're done and I'll lock up.

Standing on the rooftop, writes Michael Carroll, *fumbling with the cameras, I realized that we were in full view of the little square below. I looked down upon a knot of people all gazing indignantly up at us. With every moment their numbers, fed from the side-alleys, grew until quite a crowd stood grumbling and gesticulating below. Pushing through the crowd came a blue-coated policeman, summoned no doubt by that infernal boy by his side, wheeling the bicycle.* Carroll's ambitions are thwarted by the policeman who keeps waving his hat in front of the camera, demanding to see the 'dangerous and blaspheming' foreigner's permit to photograph mosques. Of course, he never got his shot of the mosque, but not because the policeman got his way. As Carroll tells us, *it was no good. At that moment the sun went down, almost with a bang.*

Snapping away, alone and undisturbed on the rooftop, I can imagine the scene: there is the same square below me and quite possibly the old man asleep in his chair was one of the youths who after sunset threw stones at Carroll and his Land Rover. To his credit, the Englishman took the public stoning with a stiff upper lip, but understandably decided enough was enough when a 'vandal' emerged from the bazaar with a flame-thrower. Finding the Land Rover embedded in rubble, his travelling companion David Gaunt put the engine into low-ratio gear, lurched over the stones and scattered the crowd, leaving the policeman to watch these events unfold 'uncertainly'. Carroll returned to Yazd 'of unhappy memory' later on his trip. Perhaps he was expecting trouble: on his second visit he took with him a professional boxer. They both enjoyed the magnificent beauty of the Mosque's twin minarets without taking photographs.

On balance, I think Carroll's experience of Yazd was more exciting than mine and, although I don't like people throwing stones at me, I'd quite like to have gone with him. He was a fantastic traveller and, although nowhere near as famous or popular as Byron, his book knocks *Oxiana* into a cocked hat. Bruce Chatwin would not have agreed with me. He thought Byron's book 'a sacred text, beyond criticism'. Unfortunately for Chatwin, he is wrong on both counts, unless this is simply a genteelism for 'I like it, but I don't know why... oh, wait a minute, it's all coming back to me now. We both went to Eton.' In his introduction to the Penguin Classics edition of *Oxiana*, one of the last of the 'gentleman travellers', Colin Thubron (an Old Etonian), goes into raptures over Byron's 'evocations of Persian architecture' that 'are delivered with a descriptive gift which has never been surpassed: passionately attentive, lyrical, yet almost scientifically precise.' Veteran explorer Robin Hanbury-Tenison (another Old Etonian) once told me that *Oxiana* was his favourite book. And let's not forget that it was Macmillan who first published the book in 1937. Macmillan's director of publishing at the time was the future Prime Minister, Harold, another Old Etonian. Even Paul Fussell, the distinguished literary historian, goes quite silly in the presence of Byron's book, comparing it to James Joyce's *Ulysses* and T.S. Eliot's *The Waste Land*. Perhaps he meant that he found it impossible to finish, consisting only of unrelated and uneven fragments. Don't get me wrong, I've got nothing against the Establishment closing ranks around Byron: I'm just surprised that they decided to confer greatness on such an average book.

In all fairness to Byron, it's not his fault that Chatwin liked him, and there are flashes of brilliance – diamonds in the dung if you like – that relieve the unstructured tedium of *Oxiana*. Although anthologies of Persian literature follow each other's example by quoting Byron's famous descriptions of the architecture of Esfahan (usually the Mosque of Sheikh Lutfullah), I prefer his description of the Friday Mosque in Yazd, even if it is colder and not so gorgeous.

It is hard to imagine how the portal of the Friday Mosque could escape anyone's notice. It stands over 100 feet high, and its narrow tapering arch is almost as spectacular as the chancel arch at Beauvais. After this, the court inside is a disappointment, a parochial little enclosure. But not the sanctuary, whose walls, dome, and mihrab are covered with XIVth-century mosaic in perfect condition. This is the best decoration of the kind I have seen since Herat. It differs from the work there. The colours are colder, the designs more lucid and precise, but not so gorgeous.

After an hour or so on the roof of the bazaar, I packed up my tripod and retraced my steps down the rickety stairs back to the shop, where I was hoping to thank the shop-keeper. Herodotus said of the Persians that they thought the most disgraceful thing in the world was to tell a lie, and the next worse was to owe a debt. And although I hadn't lied to the man to get onto his roof, I felt that I probably owed him a few dollars for his pains. Pulling back the curtain and blinking into the light, I noticed that the man in the black trousers and white open-necked shirt had gone. In fact everyone had gone. There was no one entering or leaving the Friday Mosque and it was as though Yazd had fallen asleep. I stuffed a large yellow 50,000-rial banknote into the nearest alms collection box and dawdled back along Emam Khomeini Avenue. The man at the spinach shop waved to me and gave me a packet of saffron.

Waiting for the sun to set in Dr Beheshti Square, I bought ice-cold melon juice from a man with a comically incontin-ent ice-cream making machine. I sat by a fountain and got talking with Marije, a Dutch woman with pale green eyes and a slightly unravelled air. She'd been travelling the Silk Road on her own for eight months and was getting annoyed with minicab drivers propositioning her. Looking at my camera, she made the universal 'you're a photographer, too' expression. I nodded and told her that I'd spent the after-noon shooting the Friday Mosque from the roof of the bazaar. 'They let you up there?' she asked. 'They told me it was not possible to go on the roof…' I shrugged and wished her *bon voyage*, fully expecting never to set eyes on her again.

But I did see Marije once more: this time deep in the mountains at Chak-Chak, a pilgrimage site for Zoroastrians. High up in a cliff-face there is a grotto containing a shrine where the sound of dripping water gives the place its name. People come here from all over Iran to pay their respects. As I listened to the water dripping into stainless steel bowls on the floor, I took a photograph of her gazing beatifically at the shrine. I later found out that I'd clumsily captured her camera strap in the photograph, clearly showing four letters of the manufacturer's logo. I'd taken an 'ikon' of the virgin Marije.

CHAPTER 20

If you want something done properly...

APUBLISHER FRIEND of mine once told me never to pay more than £80 for a book. I'm not sure how he arrived at that figure and, to judge by his private library, he almost certainly never stuck to his own advice. But his words haunt me still and whenever I'm tempted to pay upwards of this mythical integer my hands start to shake.

Irrational though it may be, this arbitrary self-imposed ceiling has often saved me from buying a book that deep down I know I don't want. On the other side of the coin, it has also provided deep satisfaction when something I bought for a song while still an undergraduate makes it past the eighty-quid barrier. It doesn't exactly make me feel like Chuck Yeager when he broke *his* barrier, but it's nice all the same.

You might wish to imagine the quandary I found myself in when photographer Henry Dallal's new book *Horse*

Warriors emerged from the stable recently at exactly £80 (there is a cheap version available for £50, but I wasn't interested in that). In terms of its editorial content it is, to say the very least, a niche title, being a pictorial essay on India's 61st Cavalry. On his acknowledgements page Dallal says that it is 'a pleasure to share with you this celebration of the splendour of India's last active horse regiment, an experience that for me has become a feast of fascination with India, its colour and magic.' Just in case Dallal needs reassurance, the pleasure is all mine, because this is a sumptuous book. I may not know much about equine pageantry, but I know a thing of beauty when I see it, and if ever there was a beautiful book then *Horse Warriors* is it. I signed the cheque with a steady hand and ripped it from its counterfoil without demur.

I like Henry Dallal's photography, and I always have done. I think he'd be a special photographer whatever he shot, but horses are his game. His first book – *Pageantry and Performance* (2003) – was a terrific photographic portrait of the Household Cavalry (familiar to most of us for their ceremonial 'Trooping the Colour'). Dallal really understands these sinewy, intelligent and handsome animals, and importantly he really understands the people who devote their lives to them. His photo-essay on the Household Cavalry is genuinely perceptive and intimate, while being the product of years of commitment to the task. How he got an 'Access All Areas' pass to a military regiment is a mystery, but it's a reflection of his dedication as a real pro. A clue may lie in his portraits of Her Majesty the Queen, which are informal and relaxed. Instead of the usual matriarchal scowl, Dallal coaxes from Queen Elizabeth a friendly smile, interpreting her formidable royal personage as a sweet, if slightly bossy, old lady. Her Majesty is known to be rather fond of Dallal's photography, so it could well be that permission came right from the top.

Pageantry and Performance might never have happened. Dallal touted his proposal around every publishing house he could think of before realising that 'no one was ever going to touch it'.

Believing that he had a book of real merit on his hands, he decided to publish it himself. This is the point where such stories normally follow a depressingly predictable path: unscrupulous vanity publishing houses fleecing the naïve and hopelessly deluded author, while countless boxes of unsold copies moulder in the cupboard under the stairs. Dallal was too clever to let this happen: he brought in corporate partners (my copy is 'In association with BAE Systems'), stayed in control of every aspect of the publication, and kept his costs stripped to the bone except for where it really mattered. At the time, London coffee table book publishers were charging big money for poorly bound titles that were printed on awful paper with repro barely better than your local newspaper. In response, Dallal single-handedly brought out a work of such high production values that it was almost embarrassing.

By his own admission he 'learned a lot' from the experience, and five years later he launched *Horse Warriors* at a glittery occasion at the Nehru Centre in Mayfair. As you might expect, there was plenty of 'book launch' wine sloshing around, while dignitaries – including Prince Michael of

Kent and the High Commissioner for India, Shri Shiv Shankar Mukherjee – enjoyed a *son et lumière* showcasing Dallal's new portfolio. A superb retrospective of Dallal's work hanging in the downstairs reception rooms provided an object lesson for anyone thinking there's no difference between digital and film photography: wall after wall of huge silky prints made from colour transparency film stock, rich and fine in texture and detail, matchless in tone and hue. Dallal's masterpieces are his equestrian silhouettes shot through the dust straight at the early morning sun. This is hard enough to accomplish on a digital camera, with limitless opportunity to shoot and reshoot while verifying your work in the field. To capture it all on film, effectively blind, without knowing what you've got in the camera, on horseback – something very few photographers have ever attempted – and to end up with these images is something special indeed.

With books like *Horse Warriors* the devil is in the detail, and Dallal is a stickler, as well as something of a showman, as we shall see. Between the foil-stamped boards there are some two hundred images beautifully reproduced on heavy, coated art paper with spot lamination on the photographs themselves as well as some of the text ornaments. The dust-jacket is folded over at both top and bottom, giving it a reassuringly expensive feel, while the interior of the slipcase has been constructed from red board to match the exterior cloth (which might be going over the top, even by Dallal's standards). Thorough chap he is, Dallal signed my copy of *Horse Warriors* twice: once on the title-page in conventional black ink, and again in a less restrained gold ink on the picture that adorns the slipcase. It's a wonderful photograph of the 61st Cavalry on early morning training manoeuvres. With a longish exposure of (something like) an eighth of a second, Dallal has managed to perfectly capture the blurred motion of the horses as the pale sunlight catches the odd bit of brass and the regimental flag.

Although he would never say so aloud, Henry Dallal's *Horse Warriors* is a triumph of individual determination: a case of 'if you want something done properly, then do it yourself'. After all this luxury and the master-class in self-publishing, disbursing the mythical sum of £80 somehow seemed more like a privilege than a debt.

Chapter 21

Yours faithfully, Ted

WHILE RECENTLY wintering in South Wales, I found myself in a gigantic book supermarket in one of those just-out-of-town shopping complexes that cluster around a car park the size of a reservoir. Now, I don't particularly dislike these developments any more than I dislike the globalised franchises that squat in them, but neither do I expect to find much in the way of literary nourishment. And yet, in Borders in Fforestfach, in amongst the whiff of Starbucks coffee, yuletide muzak and half-price ghosted autobiographies of toothless Welsh rugby players with titles like *You've Got to Try*, I found the recent *Letters of Ted Hughes*.

As I sat among the Kylie Minogue calendars reading almost every one of the 756 pages at a sitting, I realised that I'd stumbled across a book of real importance. In his introduction, editor Christopher Reid bewails that he could have produced an 'edition in three or four volumes, each just as big ... with the guarantee that no page would have been without its literary or documentary value'. If the content of this volume is anything to go by, we can believe him, although this statement is a crystal clear explanation as to why the publisher decided against calling the volume 'collected', 'selected' or even 'the' letters of Ted Hughes. Faber may well have done the decent thing by waiting for a decade to pass after the poet's death before publishing his *Letters*, but they're going to be mining this rich seam for generations to come.

Hughes' greatness ultimately rests on a highly collectable handful of early volumes of poetry, starting with *The Hawk in the Rain* (1957) and ending arguably with *Crow: From the Life and the Songs of the Crow* (1970), taking in *Lupercal* (1960) and *Wodwo* (1967) on the way. It wasn't until his swansong *Birthday Letters* (1998) that Hughes was to recapture the extraordinary muscularity of his early work.

By the 1980s, Hughes was experimenting with mixed media projects of verse and prose, collaborating with artists such as Leonard Baskin and Reg Lloyd, as well as photographers like Fay Godwin and Peter Keen. I have *Cave Birds* (1978) and *What is the Truth?* (1984), both signed by Hughes after a reading at the Oxford Union on 17th November 1984, the year in which he became Poet Laureate. However, by far my most treasured item is an early edition of *Crow* he signed that very evening, that has somehow remained in mint condition over the intervening quarter of a century. It's not a first impression of the first edition (otherwise I'd be in the market for a much-needed new car), but it is a stunning item nonetheless, with the unusual benefit of being an important literary work.

Apart from watching Hughes sign my books, my only real

recollection of the reading at the Union is the Yorkshire man growling away about an 'October salmon'. His book *River* (1983) wasn't long off the press and he was pushing this onto the clerkes of Oxenforde, who were keen to get a glimpse of the rugged-looking poet who'd famously stepped in after Philip Larkin had point-blank refused the poet laureateship. Hughes' appointment came as a surprise, because at the time Oxford was abuzz with Craig Raine, whose critically acclaimed collection of poems *Rich* (1984) had just been published by Faber. Although we couldn't possibly have known at the time, *Rich* was Raine's last proper collection of new poems (although with hindsight it's easy to see that there wasn't much petrol left in the tank: the middle section is a lengthy autobiographical prose piece, that can only have been added to make the volume substantial enough to allow the poet's name to be squeezed onto the book's spine).

From his *Letters* it's clear that Hughes liked Raine and he calls *Rich* 'your strongest collection so far', although this may simply be a little calculated flattery: Raine was an editor at Faber at the time (although *not* Hughes'), and even poets as established as Hughes can't afford to risk upsetting big publishers. At one point in *Letters* Hughes becomes quite brusque with Raine, thanking him for his 'long painstaking' criticism of the draft of (the admittedly not very important) *What is the Truth?* Tony Othen's dual studio photographic portrait of Hughes and Raine was taken around this time, and is included in the plate section of *Letters*. Even by 1980s' standards, it's appallingly embarrassing: a star-struck Raine gazes doe-like at Hughes, who is (I think) pretending to play

the piano. A much more important photograph is reproduced elsewhere in the same book: Mark Gerson's shot of a
young Hughes quaffing book launch wine with T.S. Eliot,
W.H. Auden and Stephen Spender at a Faber party in 1960
is remarkable for many reasons, especially the contrast in
their body language.

Although his literary output was patchy, and despite
being routinely trumpeted by critics as the finest poet of his
generation (he wasn't), Hughes was a proper old-fashioned
genius and I will always remember my first encounter with
him. Hughes was one of my O-level English modern poets
(along with Louis MacNeice, Hal Summers, Seamus Heaney
and Charles Causley), and I remember the indefatigable
Dr Joan Harding gently hammering a 'Thought Fox', a
jaguar and quite possibly a pike or two into us. At the time
I thought it was nonsense, but Hughes' early 'nature poetry'
shows a man completely seduced by Kipling, whom he had
devoured as a boy of fourteen: 'I fell completely under the
spell of his rhythms.' Poems that seemed so artless then
seem to have grown taproots right down to the bedrock, or,
to borrow an image from the mobile phone generation,
become hard-wired to the motherboard. If you want to
know just how good Hughes' rough-and-ready grumbling
was, revisit his 'angry' stuff. 'Do not pick up the telephone'
works even better now that we can't live without Black-
berries and the internet. This poem made it onto a short-
lived series of audiocassettes, where Faber poets read their
own work. Released in 1983, each tape showcased an establishment figure backed by a newcomer. On the 'B'-side
of Hughes' tape is the then little-known (Pulitzer prize-

winning) Paul Muldoon, whose subtle and charming *Quoof* was published in the same year.

But I digress. Having gone up to Oxford to read English, I once again encountered the gravelly poet, only this time as Mr Sylvia Plath. Plath was posthumously enjoying something of a revival, and at the time it was fashionable for militant feminists to despise Hughes on the basis that he had 'murdered' his wife (the exact location of Hughes' memorial was originally kept a secret for fear that feminists would deface it). *Letters* makes clear that anyone who came into contact with Plath lived in fear of the 'approaching storm' and its consequences. Knowing what we know now, it's amazing that Hughes managed to refrain from being drawn into full-scale battle on the subject, although there are times when the old dog barks a bit. In one letter to a broadsheet newspaper in the seventies, he states outright that an article by two American Plath scholars libels him. But he doesn't go much further, claiming that he is no expert on the academic debate about Plath that had by then spawned 700 articles and books.

For those who have fallen into the trap of thinking that Hughes was a curmudgeonly lump of granite leaving a trail of human misery in his wake, the wide-ranging brilliance of his correspondence will come as a welcome surprise. We tend to forget Hughes' prowess as a critic, storyteller, essayist and thinker, and we overlook his sheer technical expertise with language, expressing complex thoughts with resonant lucidity. A bigger surprise is the warmth that he radiates: at the end of a long letter to his daughter Frieda, containing crib notes about Cleopatra and Julius Caesar, there is a postscript in which he asks for the name of her English teacher. Hughes wants to thank him for 'sending those poems'. You can almost hear father and daughter squealing with conspiratorial delight. In the final letter of the volume, written nine days before his death, he writes to his Aunt Hilda, describing a visit to Buckingham Palace to receive the Order of Merit. He recalls how, on presenting the Queen with a copy of *Birthday Letters*, 'she was fascinated' and 'extremely vivacious & happy-spirited'. Hughes, it seemed, could communicate with anyone. As Seamus Heaney said at the poet's funeral: 'No death in my lifetime has hurt poets more… His creative powers were, as Shakespeare said, still crescent. By his death, the veil of poetry is rent and the walls of learning broken.'

Borders in Fforestfach closed its doors on the reading public of South Wales for the last time over the Christmas 2009 holiday season, following the collapse of the chain bookseller.

CHAPTER 22

Letter from America

I T'S NOT EVERY day you watch an aeroplane fall out of the sky, but on 15th January 2009 at 3:31pm local time, as I was walking down New York's West Side, this is exactly what I saw. I didn't witness the point of contact between the Airbus A320 and the Hudson River because there were several tall buildings in the way, but I did hear the squawking sirens of countless ambulances, police cars, fire engines and other emergency vehicles as they raced to the Hudson's banks. New York's collective initial reaction was that this was the work of Al-Qaeda and it was 9/11 all over again. As the story unfolded and it became clear that the 'Miracle on the Hudson' was a well-executed emergency landing after a low-altitude collision with a flock of Canada geese, the city settled into slapping itself on the back, to the beery cheers of 'God Bless America', while declaring the pilot of Flight 1549 – Chesley Burnett 'Sully' Sullenberger III – a national hero.

Feeling the need for what Bertie Wooster might call a 'restorative', I dropped anchor at the White Horse Tavern on

Hudson Street. The White Horse is an old longshoreman's watering hole that briefly became popular with the Big Apple's literati in the 1950s, but is famous today as the place where Dylan Thomas drank his last, hanging up his drinking trousers after a session taking in an alleged eighteen straight whiskies. 'I think it's a record', he's supposed to have said a week before dying of what the pathologist's report described as 'an insult to the brain'. The only undisputed fact in the controversy that surrounds Thomas's death seems to be that the White Horse was a favourite with the Welsh poet.

Other quill-wielding clients included Norman Mailer, Jack Kerouac and Hunter S. Thompson. But it's hard to see what the attraction might have been to such men of letters today when the bar is lined with huge plasma screens broadcasting endless reruns of baseball, basketball and football, their sound muted while piped 'adult-oriented rock' closes down any remaining intellectual reflexes. Don't get me wrong, I like American football (as did Alistair Cook, who despised the British habit of dismissing it out of hand), but I didn't come to New York to watch television.

Wandering back towards my hotel in Midtown I became hopelessly lost, and despite the mercury having fallen to -20C I ended up doing what every visitor does: late night window-shopping. By far the most interesting window is on the corner of Madison Avenue and East 35th Street, where I encountered the Complete Traveller antiquarian bookstore. I made a mental note to return, recalibrated my course, set off north-west and promptly found myself in a street boasting three of what the guidebooks call 'old-time bars': the Ginger Man, the Galway Hooker and Slattery's

Roadside bar in the Caribbean, where the idea for 'Coronation Cricket' formed after an afternoon with a cabbie who'd been Andrew Flintoff's driver during the notorious 'Fredalo' scandal.
(Chapter 12)

Pink pigeon in Mauritius, once one of the rarest birds on the planet, that gave the title to Gerald Durrell's book *Golden Bats and Pink Pigeons*.
(Chapter 15)

Antiquarian bookshop in London's Cecil Court,
perhaps the finest street for books in the world.
(Passim)

The inaugural meeting of the G.H. Mumm Champagne Cordon Rouge Club
at the Royal Geographical Society, 2008.
Chairman Bear Grylls is in pink linen.
(Chapter 16)
(By permission G.H. Mumm Champagne)

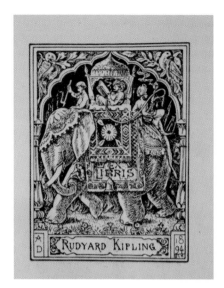

Title-page and ownership bookplate on Rudyard Kipling's copy of *The South Polar Times* at the National Maritime Museum. *(Chapter 18)*

The Friday Mosque in Yazd, Iran, once photographed by Robert Byron and almost photographed by Michael Carroll. Today it's hard to get a clear shot. *(Chapter 19)*

Above: Village Cigars in New York, taken on 15th January 2009, the day of the 'Miracle on the Hudson'. *(Chapter 22)*

Left: 'Ikon' of a woman traveller at Chak-Chak in central Iran. *(Chapter 19)*

Wide-angle 'floor shot' up a mature elephant's trunk. *(Chapter 25)*

Injured leopard in Botswana's Okavango Delta.
Not a man-eater, but quite possibly as dangerous as
those shot by Jim Corbett.
(*Chapter 25*)

Neil Armstrong and Buzz Aldrin on the surface of the Moon
during their *Apollo 11* expedition (posed by models).
(*Chapter 27*)

The author at a ceremonial North Pole, a few miles away from 90 degrees north. *(Chapter 28)*
(Photo: Sue Flood)

Polar bear on the Arctic ice close to Franz Josef Land, Russia. *(Chapter 28)*

A bookshop inside the old railway station in Damascus in Syria,
with strong associations with T.E. Lawrence and the Arab Revolt.
(Chapter 31)

Journey's start and end. The beach at Jambiani in Zanzibar
where the author started and finished his four-year trip around the world
with the seafaring novels of Patrick O'Brian.
(Chapter 32)

Above: 'I had a farm in Africa at the foot of the Ngong Hills.' Karen Blixen's coffee farm in suburban Nairobi. *(Chapter 35)*

Left: Part of a herd of more than a hundred elephants at Ol Malo, Northern Kenya. *(Chapter 35)*

The compass that Shackleton took with him to his farthest South on the *Nimrod* expedition of 1907-09. *(Appendix 2)*

Midtown Pub. Opting for the least poetic of these I soon found myself in conversation with an Irish barman who was simultaneously having a good-natured argument with his regulars about the 'Miracle on the Hudson'. 'We don't hate Canadians, man,' said a student who looked scarily like a young Stephen King with a jazz beard: 'It's just that their geese brought down our airplane, man.' With regulars like this you can see why Slattery's opted to keep their name nice and simple. You can communicate to your yellow cab driver the address, district and what you're going to do in three simple words. It's so prosaic and compact it borders on genius.

The Complete Traveller antiquarian bookstore started off selling any new travel book in existence, its proprietor Arnold L. Greenberg told me the following morning. 'Little by little I started to add some old books. There were some Baedekers scattered here and there and after a while the old books became even with the new books. Little by little we got rid of the new books completely and started dealing exclusively with old books and that's where we are today.' I ask him how the global recession is affecting business. 'Sure. Fewer people are coming in. Our best barometer is the number of phone calls we get from people trying to sell us books, rather than from people who want to buy them. People sell books in bad times. People don't sell books when things are hunky-dory.'

Greenberg says he has the best stock of Baedekers 'in the western hemisphere. There's a gentleman in London called Bernard Shapero who has maybe more, but if you want a Baedeker you generally would go there or hopefully here.'

Apart from the Baedekers and what he calls 'Baedeker clones', Greenberg has a tremendous collection of WPA (Works Progress Administration) books that were published during the Depression and the 1940s. Part of the programme was a scheme to get unemployed writers into employment, and big names to emerge include Ralph Ellison, Richard Wright, and Studs Turkel. 'I think Steinbeck was in there somewhere,' says Greenberg. 'Writers who had been on relief of $10 a month were suddenly making $200 for doing what they loved. And the books were profitable.'

Greenberg's third speciality is the A. &. C. Black 20/- Colour Books series. Of the 92 titles, Greenberg generally has sixty or seventy in stock. The 20/- series was published in the Edwardian era between 1901 and 1921, a Golden Age for book illustrations. Although photography was established, the black-and-white images couldn't hold a candle to Arthur Rackham and Edmund Dulac, and with most volumes having seventy or more colour plates, 'they make beautiful gifts. They sell really well, especially around Christmas.'

Because of its location on Madison, the Complete Traveller has an eclectic mix of customers. 'We get a lot of people who have no intention of buying anything. We call them tyre-kickers, after the guys who go to a car sales court. You know they're not going to buy, but they're kicking the tyres, looking like they know what they're doing.' Greenberg recalls the story of a customer who came in ecstatic that he had finally found the book he'd been after for many years. 'He was so happy. He was saying, "My God, I can't believe it. After eight years of searching I have finally found it. I can't

believe this is my day – it's the most important thing in my life." So he asked me how much it was, and I told him $75. And he looked at me and said, "I'm not paying that for it." '
He's slightly more impressed that Salman Rushdie dropped in recently, as did Mario Vargas Llosa and a 'pretty actress. You know, the one John F. Kennedy Jr didn't marry.'

Greenberg tells me that the Complete Traveller became exclusively an antiquarian concern 'just about the time of 9/11. Things were getting bad with the superstores discounting travel books, and the internet was getting more influential. And then one day somebody walked in and asked if it was safe to go to Boston, so we knew we weren't going to sell a lot of books on Sumatra. So that was it. Nobody wanted to travel anymore. Goodbye.' With promises to return to the Complete Traveller on my next visit to New York, I said goodbye to Arnold L. Greenberg, clutching a beautiful copy of *Persia: the Awakening East* by W.P. Cresson FRGS, published by J.B. Lippincott in 1908. Not common, it is even nicer in that it is inscribed 'to Richard Renshaw Neil esq, from his friend the author, December 1910.'

No literary tour of New York would be complete without a stroll in Central Park, where the famous Literary Walk has statues erected to honour the memories of such greats as William Shakespeare, Sir Walter Scott, Robert Burns and Fitz-Greene Halleck. If the last of these names seems to sit a little awkwardly with the remainder of the company, it's worth remembering that Halleck was once 'the American Byron', one of America's greatest poets and much admired by Charles Dickens. In 1877 his statue was dedicated by

US president Rutherford B. Hayes in front of a cheering crowd of (according to contemporary newspaper reports) ten thousand enthusiasts for the poet, whose books were in such demand that regular editions routinely went on sale for as much as twenty times their normal price.

Halleck's is a cautionary tale of the transitory nature of fame and fortune, and one that today's celebrity-obsessed world would do well to consider. In 2006 the Fitz-Greene Halleck Society was founded to honour and remember this forgotten literary Titan or, as the society Eliotically puts it, 'the memory of the forgetting'. Of course there are plenty of editions of Halleck in print, and even a biography or two, but the fact remains that he hasn't aged anywhere near as well as Shakespeare, Scott or Burns. And yet, if the words of Napoleon are true – 'fame is fleeting, obscurity is forever' – then Halleck is one of the immortals, his place on at least the nursery slopes of Parnassus guaranteed for eternity.

CHAPTER 23

When the going gets tough

O NE OF THE yardsticks economists use to define a
recession is that of two consecutive quarters of
negative growth in the economy. Doubtless there
are plenty of people who would argue with this: I sat next
to a markets analyst on a flight to Frankfurt recently, who
lectured me for an hour on why he thought the recession is
a myth. But for us book people, who look no further for our
economic information than the business pages of the *Daily
Telegraph*, it's the one we're most used to, and we should
probably stick with it. However, you know when you've been
entrenched in an economic slump too long when, instead
of reading about it in the broadsheet dailies, you're reading
about it in books.

New books have notoriously long lead-times, so when I
received one recently that appeared to have been written
specifically to aid business survival in the 'current climate'
(whatever that means), I started to wonder if the recession

has been with us for longer than strictly necessary. Called *Tough Tactics for Tough Times* and subtitled no less alarmingly 'How to Maintain Business in Difficult Economic Conditions', I originally thought that this offering from authors Patrick Forsyth and Frances Kay might be a reprint of something published in the early 1990s, when the *Economist* was all about 'negative equity' rather than 'quantitative easing'. But no, it's a new book, and with entrepreneurial flair not normally associated with the trade its publisher, Kogan Page, has managed to rush a book to market that is relevant and for the most part useful.

I qualify 'useful' because it's one of those truths not universally acknowledged that the people who read management books are those who don't need to. It follows that sensible employers, who care about the welfare of their staff, suppliers and customers, will turn to *Tough Tactics for Tough Times* and come away saying, 'But I know all that.' It's a sad fact of life that the bosses who most need training in management skills are the ones who declare themselves too busy to read books like this. This is a shame because I've worked for several spivs who really do need a copy of this book under their pillow. I'd like to name and shame them in *Travels in the World of Books*, but a quick phone call to my lawyer revealed that this would be a bad idea. There will be useless idiots in senior management roles until the end of time, so there's no point getting annoyed about it, but I just can't help feeling that the worthy Forsyth and Kay are preaching to the converted.

However, it is worth turning to *Tough Tactics for Tough Times* for more than a superficial skim, not so much for the advice it dispenses, but for the defiant tone in which it is offered. Not for Forsyth and Kay the touchy-feely language of inclusivity and polite suggestion. This is a broadside volley, leaving the reader under no illusion that, if you're to make it through the recession and come out the other side in one piece, 'hoping for the best' is not an option. You need to do something, say the authors, and you need to do it now, because if you sit on your hands you'll go out of business. I'm guessing that this advice applies as much to the world of books as to anywhere else.

Given that the central tenet is so apocalyptic, it comes as no surprise that some of the advice given is pretty ruthless (actually, some of it is unconscionable, but don't get me started on management ethics). The way to avoid wasting time dealing with mountains of unwanted paperwork, say the authors, is simply to delegate. But isn't that just wasting somebody else's time? Too bad. Go back to the title – these are *Tough Tactics for Tough Times*. Why waste energy, ask the authors, travelling to see a client, when the client could come to you? Well, yes, but isn't that merely bumping a problem along rather than solving it? Tough luck, say the authors, these are *Tough Tactics for Tough Times*. And so it goes on. When chasing up payments over the phone, stand up. Why? Because you'll be more assertive (read 'aggressive') and instead of mildly apologising for the interruption you'll cut to the chase, demand your money and be back in business before you can say Jack Robinson. If that lacks some of the citizenship values required by civilised society then tough, these are ... you get the message.

Despite my natural inclination to recoil from anything

remotely resembling confrontation, I was greatly impressed by one piece of advice on how to prioritise your 'to-do' list. Write your list they say, and grade your tasks 'A' and 'B', where A-tasks are the more important. Then carefully tear off the B-section, crumple it up into a ball and toss it into the waste-paper basket. While part of me would like to think that this is symbolic, the logician in me likes this uncompromising approach a lot. It may sound obvious, but if you only have time to do half of your jobs, make sure the half you get around to is the important half. 'Become a list freak,' they say ... believe me, if you follow this advice, you'll be called names more colourful than 'freak'.

But I digress. Underlying the book's strategy is the assumption that we are all prone to wasting time and that none of us is as adept at time management as we'd like to think. As if to emphasise this, the authors present their ideas in something of a staccato style, presumably justified by the rationale that today's busy businessman is too busy transacting business to bother reading books on how to do it properly or responsibly. And while I admire the authors' technique, this bullet-point approach to complex issues can fall foul of over-simplifying issues that simply can't be expressed in black-and-white terms. In their section about cutting travel costs, the authors take the sensible view that air travel is an overused resource. Interestingly, their only concern is the cost in financial terms and nowhere do they consider the environmental consequences of overseas business travel, but we'll let that pass (as the authors might say, 'It is outside our brief'). Don't fly Business Class, the authors intone with Blairite piety, because it's expensive and will cause resentment elsewhere in your business where the chocolate biscuits have been axed. Well, yes and no. First, your business is not a democracy, while the whole point of Business Class is to allow people of commerce to work while they are in transit, so that they maximise their utility to the organisation that pays their salt. If you spend a 7-hour flight from London to New York squashed in economy (or World Traveller, or some such nonsense), where you can't even manage a crossword, then what profit is there in that? In Business Class you might appear to be quaffing bubbly on the company's tab, but this is of no importance if while airborne you've written and dispatched quotations to the tune of several thousands of pounds. The real question is not how expensive your flight is, but what are your reasons for travelling? Too many flights are taken on a flimsy pretext – New York Antiquarian Book Fair? – say the authors, because of the warm glow we get from having a passport full of exotic entry visas.

At the beginning of *Tough Tactics for Tough Times* Forsyth and Kay quote the American comedian Lily Tomlin: 'Things are going to get a lot worse before they get worse.' I think we can all agree that for a comedian that's not particularly funny, but it sets the tone of the text, which unequivocally says that for things to get worse all that is required is for you to do nothing (which sounds suspiciously like Edmund Burke's 'All that is required for evil to prevail is for good men to do nothing.') Having said that, within a few pages we're referred to another comedian of sorts, the writer Douglas Adams, who in his *Hitch-hiker's Guide to the Galaxy* famously urged us not to panic (which sounds suspiciously like Lance-Corporal Jones in *Dad's Army*). Remarkably, these two ideas combine to form the central theme of *Tough Tactics for Tough Times*. It's one of those 'if you only read one thing' moments and the authors are entirely correct in deriving much of their advice from the simple formula of staying calm while taking action. That action, say the authors, depends on who you are, who your customers are, and what the prevailing business conditions are. But, if you sit there hoping that things can only get better, you'll soon find yourself up a certain creek without an instrument of propulsion. Hardly advice in any positive sense, but worth listening to all the same.

CHAPTER 24

Airborne with Isabel

Y OU KNOW WHEN you've been travelling too much
when you no longer care what the time is and you
start to think that everything can be dealt with in
American dollars, even in London. I've been to Vancouver,
Frankfurt, Abu Dhabi and Stevenage, all in the space of a
month. Had it not been for my constant travelling companion – the wonderful Isabel Dalhousie – I might have
found it a chore.

Isabel is of course fictional. She's the well-heeled, professional philosopher who gives her name to the series of
Alexander McCall Smith's novels that have titles such as *The
Sunday Philosophy Club*, *The Right Attitude to Rain* and
The Careful Use of Compliments. I'd been thinking of
reading them for a while but, put off by their covers, I've
allowed them to languish on the 'not very probable' pile.
Conventional wisdom has it that you shouldn't judge a book
by its cover, but since Adam McCauley's stylishly evocative
designs appear to propel Isabel unashamedly towards the
'mozzarella and sun-dried tomatoes' sector, I fell foul of

the trap. Until now I'd taken the expression to be meta-
phorical, and never really suspected it could be applied to
actual books. And yet, faced with a half-stocked Borders in
Heathrow, I decided to grab a couple of paperback Isabels
and give her a whirl, covers notwithstanding.

The Isabel Dalhousie novels are deceptively light com-
edies of manners set in Edinburgh, McCall Smith's home-
town. Unlike the author's fantastically popular *No 1 Ladies
Detective Agency* series, which is implicitly about moral
philosophy, these books are *explicitly* about moral philosophy. His protagonist is editor of the quarterly *Review of
Applied Ethics*, a journal that provides the serving spoon
with which to dish up the moral dilemmas that confront
Isabel and the ensemble cast of mostly well-to-do, well-
educated white Scotsmen and women. Although this may
seem light years away from Mma Ramotswe's Botswana, the
two series share the core concern of how to reach an understanding of proper human behaviour (another similarity is
that the heroines of both employ a sidekick called Grace).
I read recently in *The Ethical Executive* by Robert Hoyk
and Paul Hersey that one definition of such behaviour is
that which hurts no one while being of potential benefit to
all: what game theorists call the 'non-zero sum' result.
Resolving conflicts of interest with this outcome in mind is
what Isabel Dalhousie, as both philosopher and human
being, is striving to achieve, and this is what supplies these
books with their plots.

After several days airborne with Isabel I confess myself
deeply attracted to her. I disagree sharply with critics who
find her wealth, moral integrity and beauty a little too good

to be true. I find her fascinating *precisely* because she is perfect, as well as enjoying the comparative novelty of a central character without a tragic flaw. To include a plotline where a 40-something divorcee – no matter how visually splendid – can bag herself a 'beautiful' 28-year-old bassoonist shows McCall Smith's knack of demonstrating how predictable currents of probability can have an unexpected undertow. And yet it is her generosity of spirit, rather than her wealth or looks, that makes her so attractive. She is undeniably extremely rich by any standards, which is not in any sense a virtue, but she is anonymously philanthropic, which certainly is.

We also like her because she allows a fox to live in her garden, where it rears its young under the shed. Brother Fox is a moral test for the reader. Why would Isabel allow a fox to live in her garden when you'd have Rentokil around to exterminate it faster than you could say knife? The answer is, she's inherently good: the sort of person who instinctively and deliberately cares for people who are emotionally less well off than her, for whom goodness is literally the day-job.

It would be nice to say that I've got a lot in common with Isabel, but she is, alas (for me at least) an inspirational character. But I do have plenty of sympathy with her as a professional journalist. As editor of the *Review of Applied Ethics* she has her imperfections, occasionally overstepping her remit by straying into the territory of moral theory, much to the self-satisfied irritation of some members of the publication's editorial board. Again, I sympathise: I don't claim to be an expert in moral philosophy, but I have edited more than my fair share of monthly magazines and I know that the most time-consuming issue, requiring the most diplomatic agility, is that of dealing with 'the constituency'. For those thinking the duties of the modern magazine editor mainly consist of literary luncheons in Bloomsbury, or checking the Test Match score online while flicking through a file of press releases from Faber & Faber, light sauternes to hand, the truth will be a rude awakening. The grubby reality is that the job is a defensive role, where much time is spent fending off offensive skirmishes from the Awkward Squad, be they in the form of advertisers, contributors, editorial board members, publishers or even readers.

Usually I deal with professional journalists, seasoned hacks who know the ropes, who'll chop you out 800 print-ready words before you can say 'double whisky'. They can be a trying bunch, so I can only imagine Isabel's life as an editor of a peer-reviewed academic journal, whose contributors appear to be driven by motives more greedy and devious even than the pursuit of money or alcohol. Their need to publish is not fuelled by the desire to contribute to the canon of ethics, to bequeath their wisdom to future generations, or even to cast light on the thornier points of current philosophical thinking. It is triggered by the need to draw attention to the self, to rack up wordage in order to climb the academic ladder, or to carve a notch on the academic bedpost, during the execution of which, if an arch rival becomes irked or jealous, so much the better.

Pity the poor editor. Isabel spends much of her time reading unsolicited paper manuscripts (she refuses to read electronic submissions on her computer screen, forcing her into the very modern moral circle of hell called sustainability). Most of what she receives is borderline at best, such as a paper entitled 'The Concept of Sexual Perversion as an Oppressive Weapon', which doesn't make it into print, or 'On the Ethics of Pretending to be Gay When You Are Not', which does, despite being a straightforward disquisition on lying, while pretending not to be. Then there are the papers submitted by PhD students, post-docs and other junior academics that have no realistic chance of making it into the *Review of Applied Ethics*. Before rejecting their work, Isabel treats these self-deluded souls thoughtfully, despite their uninvited arrival in her 'moral proximity'. Although she is too polite to say so, this is amateur jetsam from what a former colleague on a magazine in the Isle of Dogs used to call 'the green Biro brigade'.

Politeness is, of course, what sets McCall Smith's books apart. Over the past few years I've read nigh on two dozen of his novels and not once have I encountered so much as a syllable that would make a nun blush. His style is understated, breezy and polite – perhaps too polite, as I find myself serenaded into allowing his use of the formal third person singular, which one normally detests. Even when Isabel and Jamie (her 28-year-old bassoonist) consummate their affections in a country house in Scotland, there is a discreet cutaway to the morning after, with only a brief flashback to explain how they got there. Their love is that of 'Eros', while their union is symbolised by the housekeeper needing to resupply only one of their rooms the following morning with a fresh bottle of water.

That McCall Smith can get away with such lightness of touch, when we're told the public demands ever more extremes of explicitness, confirms my long-held belief (and I suspect his too) that, while sex may sell, some things are more important to the success of a novel, both in creative and commercial terms. And, because he never underestimates his reader, he rightly assumes they will think so too. When *The Right Attitude to Rain* is adapted for television it will inevitably be treated with a heavy hand by producers who, thinking they know better, will crank up the raunch factor in an attempt to reach a wider audience. Of course I can't be sure that this is exactly what will happen, but there is plenty of form.

Somewhere 35,000 feet above the Canadian Shield I snap shut *The Comfort of Saturdays*, switch on the in-flight entertainment and wait for lunch to arrive. They're rerunning Andrew Davies's 1995 adaptation of *Pride and Prejudice*, the one where Colin Firth as Fitzwilliam Darcy famously takes off his shirt. If I'm being charitable, the best I can say is it's not particularly good. But TV adaptations never are because their producers always want consumer-digestible, zeitgeisty piffle no matter what the directors have in mind. It occurs to me that, with each successive television incarnation of Jane Austen's heroine, the amplitude and acreage of Eliza Bennet's décolletage increases in inverse proportion to the editorial attention paid to the moral and social concerns of the novel. This is particularly sad because it is Austen's almost imperceptible rebellions, rather than the pulchritude of her women, that make *Pride and Prejudice* so naughty in the first place. Travesties of interpretation such as this are

not simply an error of professional or even literary judge-
ment on the part of the television hacks, but an ethical issue
concerned with how far we should be allowed to distort a
classic in order to make it acceptable to a mass audience –
a debate I feel certain that Isabel, for all her almost saintly
perfections, would find impossible to resist.

CHAPTER 25

Hunter home from
the hill

A FEW YEARS ago I received a phone call from a publisher asking if I'd like to abridge a book for him. Although I'd edited countless magazines and considered myself a dab hand at reducing virtually any tract of text to almost nothing, I'd never truncated a book in this fashion and had no idea what was involved, or where even to start. I hadn't read many abridgements, but those I had were mostly abject, like thoroughbred racehorses filleted with a lump of rusty metal. Without a moment's hesitation I replied in the affirmative.

The book in question was *The Man-Eating Leopard of Rudraprayag*, Jim Corbett's between-the-wars tale of derring-do in the far-flung jungle outposts of Imperial India. This was a time when gentlemen soldiers with handlebar moustaches stalked big cats for months on end before shooting them between the eyes. You either like this sort of book or you don't, and I personally wouldn't blame anyone for hating any account that made entertainment of the slaughter of innocent animals. But the man-eater of Rudraprayag was far from innocent. It had killed 125 Indians, striking fear into a nation, and the evil feline had to go. The legendary Corbett was the man for the job and this is his tale.

With a career total of 19 tigers and 14 leopards under his belt, Corbett was in no way as bloody as some of the classic 'great white hunters' such as Frederick Courteney Selous, who by the age of 25 had become the world's most famous professional elephant hunter and notorious in the international ivory trade. (With what some might consider poetic justice, Selous was killed in 1917 by a sniper's bullet in an engagement at Beho Beho in German East Africa during the Great War. Quite what the 67-year-old was doing on the front-line in the riparian savannah fighting the Bosch is for the historians to discover. But I do know– because I've been there – that he was buried near to where he fell under a tamarind tree close to the Hot Springs in what is now the Selous Game Reserve in modern Tanzania.)

Unlike the 'Mighty Nimrod', as Selous became known, Corbett only killed animals that needed killing (the main reason being their threat to human settlements) and he claimed that he took no pleasure in their despatch other than that of a job well done. He deeply regretted an incident where he had shot a 'normal' leopard under the mistaken impression that it was a man-eater. Despite his later conversion to the causes of conservation and wildlife photography, Corbett was in some ways simply Kipling with a gun. Regarded by the people of India's Kumaon region as a *sadhu*, he was also, as his friend Lord Hailey wrote, 'one of the small band of Europeans whose memory has been worshipped by Indians as that of men who were in some measure also gods.'

My commission was to abridge the original text of *The Man-Eating Leopard of Rudraprayag* from what looked like somewhere in the region of 40,000 words to a mere 8,000. Although mental arithmetic is not my strong point, it appeared to me that I was to reduce a work of considerable craft (if not art) to a fifth of its original size. I decided that in order to achieve the required cuts I'd have to be absolutely ruthless. I also decided that for the resulting manuscript to bear any resemblance to Corbett's work I'd need to resist the temptation to sub edit, write link pieces or use elision. In short, my mission was to execute the reduction by cutting passages in their entirety, relying on the integrity of the original story and the intelligence of the reader to provide a unified whole.

As I prepared to carve up *The Man-Eating Leopard of Rudraprayag* I remembered the words of my English master at Olchfa Comprehensive School in Swansea, who once told me that I'd never know any work of literature deeper or better than I would come to know my A-Level set texts. Mr George – now Phil George, Creative Director of an independent TV production company and Chair of National Theatre Wales – was doing an inspired job instilling *The Mill on the Floss, The Return of the Native* and *Women in Love* into a small class of receptive but easily distracted brains, preparing us for our A-levels back in the early 1980s. And while I bow to Mr George in all matters related to the teaching of English literature, I'm afraid I have to inform him that I'm now sadly better acquainted with

The Man-Eating Leopard of Rudraprayag than I am with either *The Tempest* or *Antony and Cleopatra*.

Fortunately for me, *Rudraprayag* is one of those episodic linear narratives by a man more proficient with a shotgun than with the typewriter and as such it lends itself to open-heart surgery without much fear of what the consequences may be. Whatever you do, it will end up action-packed, tense and exciting. With no sub-plots or discernible literary artifice to slow me down, I had high hopes of getting to the Oval and being tucked into a pint of Young's by lunchtime.

I bought myself an OUP (India) paperback copy on the internet for £3.99 and, armed with nothing more than a 2B pencil and a highlighter pen, started work. As I said earlier, I had absolutely no idea of what I was doing, and had I appreciated how delicately complex the task was going to be I might not have been so gung-ho. I struck out the paragraphs I definitely didn't want and encircled the ones I did. After several passes back and forth I managed, by process of deduction and instinct, to work out how to keep in the best bits while maintaining some sort of narrative continuity. The idea was that I'd eventually end up with four times more graphite than yellow fluorescent ink, at which point I'd have the core of my version of *Rudraprayag*. Having bashed it into the laptop I could then go about the business of preparing the text for publication.

By the time I'd worked on the manuscript for a week I'd managed to produce a crisp, clean and quite likeable version of Corbett's classic. Of course, I'd completely ruined it. Corbett's books aren't meant to be crisp, clean and quite likeable at all. As with so much non-fiction of the time, they're supposed to be educational, morally uplifting and a lesson on how to write in the style of the Georgian and, as we shall see, Elizabethan withdrawing room. Above all, his books are extraordinarily addictive and I idled away several days reading his other works, labouring under the delusion that this was research, an immersion into the world of the sub-continental jungle that would prepare the artistic scalpel to make excisions of great grace.

Since completing the abridgement of *Rudraprayag* I've made a half-hearted attempt to collect Corbett. There are two main benefits in such an enterprise: first, he only wrote six books; and second, they're all reasonably gettable, with no black tulips in the portfolio. For my money Corbett's best book is his first, *Man-Eaters of Kumaon* (1944). My version is an early one, scruffy and with the dust-jacket in pieces, but I love the ownership inscription on the front endpaper that tells me it once belonged to Major J.H. McCulloch of 'Agra, India'. Even more fantastic is the title-page where the words 'Well met in the jungle' appear in the major's hand, although in a different colour ink. I'm not sure if this qualifies as an association copy, but it's a fascinating object, even if it's worth next to nothing.

There seem to be very few autographed copies of Corbett's work around at the moment and so when I saw a signed first of *The Temple Tiger and more man-eaters of Kumaon* (1954) recently at an antiquarian book fair at the Royal Geographical Society the hands started to shake a little. Although it was fairly battered – I've yet to see any Corbetts in good condition – it wasn't a total wreck, and the spidery inscription in blue Biro seemed to add something indefinable in the way that signatures sometimes can. I started to think carefully about disbursing the three-figure sum required to separate it from its owner, but was brought back to earth by a comment from the seller. Corbett had signed the book in January 1955 and I pointed out that this was a mere three months before his death in Kenya, and so it was conceivable that the copy was one of the last he ever signed. 'Oh yes', came the reply, 'but he definitely signed it *before* he died.' Er, quite.

Corbett's sixth and last book was a slender volume called *Tree Tops*. Published posthumously in 1955, it is his account of the visit of the then heir to the British throne and her recently acquired husband Prince Philip to the arboreal lookout post in the Kenyan grasslands. The year was 1952, and he describes in great detail the all-round pluckiness of Princess Elizabeth, to whom he is hopelessly devoted. In those days it was fashionable for the great and the good to dispense 'libation of saline' (a bucket of salt water) to attract wildlife and, as a consequence, on Elizabeth's arrival there was a nervous herd of elephant loitering at the foot of the ladder that led to the *machan* or viewing platform. The young princess, according to Corbett, squared her regal shoulders and walked bravely past the impertinent pachyderms (where was F.C. Selous when you needed him?).

To say that *Tree Tops* is reverential in tone is to wildly understate Corbett's respect for royalty. Today, it's easy to think of Corbett's style as sycophantic or obsequious, but the opportunity to sup with the future Queen of England in a tree house in the middle of Kenya was a 'day of days', and I can hardly blame him for saying so.

Perhaps this is because I travelled through Kenya in the late 1990s and recognise much of the landscape of Corbett's text. I also spent the night at Tree Tops in the Aberdare National Park and, like Princess Elizabeth, I spent exactly twenty hours there. You arrive at 2pm and leave by 10am the following day. These days they do their best to make it a colonial experience, but the truth is that you're bused in and the viewing platform that you ascend to in the Cape Chestnuts isn't the original Elizabeth watched elephants from – African Guerrillas burnt that down in the 1954 Mau Mau uprising (although you can still see traces of it on the other side of the waterhole). Today's version is much more commercial, with fifty bedrooms, a pay bar and a 1,000-Watt artificial moon.

Elizabeth's father, George VI, died during the night of her stay at Tree Tops, where a young woman climbed a gigantic Ficus tree a princess and came down a queen. This saying has now passed into the language and is used and misused so often it is probable that many will be neither aware that it was Corbett who coined the phrase nor what the exact words are. Like many upper-crust game lodges, Tree Tops kept (and still did a decade ago) a visitors' book in which to write observations of white rhino, bushbuck, warthog and even the occasional leopard. But the septuagenarian Corbett had higher things on his mind as he wiped a tear from his eye and said goodbye to his Sovereign before writing:

> For the first time in the history of the world a young girl climbed into a tree one day a princess, and after having what she described as her most thrilling experience she climbed down from the tree the next day a Queen – God bless her.

152

CHAPTER 26

Whatever happened to the infotainment stubby?

Y EARS OF WORKING from home have taught me that you should never do anything more compli- cated than lounge around with a cup of tea between 11:00 and noon. This is the time the postman calls with his daily variety of padded envelopes containing proofs, catalogues and all sorts of other printed material ultimately destined for the orange recycling bag that sits at the top of the stairway to my cellar. If you miss the postman you end up with several of those dreary red-and-white forms that accuse you of being out, while you were in fact on the phone, and the packets end up in a warehouse in Belfast. My postman tells me that, if they remain uncollected for more than a week, they are automatically returned to their sender, and so the cycle starts all over again. Given that I live in south London and am unprepared to make a special trip to Northern Ireland simply to pick up a few 'advanced information' notices and the odd invitation to drink warm chardonnay at a book-signing, the cycle churns with something bordering on monotony.

And so most mornings as I toil at the iMac, watching the squirrels run up and down the apple tree, at around 11 o'clock I go on red alert. It's become a challenge to get to the door before the postman redirects my mail to the Emerald Isle. The ceremonial opening of the parcels that follows is normally one that leads to disappointment, and yet a week ago there was the unexpected pleasure of a proof copy of *Poseidon's Steed* by the unknown Helen Scales PhD. In short, it is one of those beautiful little books that come along only every now and then. It's well written, nicely researched, interesting and, best of all, it's about seahorses. If her debut is anything to go by she won't be unknown for long, and we can look forward to plenty more from this talented newcomer. Her publisher is Gotham Books in the United States, and as yet there is no British publication scheduled, which is a shame because this confirms my suspicion that here in Blighty we've turned our back on one of the great publishing phenomena of the late 1990s.

At that time I was the editor of a popular science magazine, and one of my first moves on taking up the chair was to increase the extent of the book review section. Good high-concept non-fiction was abundant in those days, with barely a month going by without the likes of Stephen Pinker, Steve Jones, Stephen Jay Gould and a whole host of other Stephens delivering a literary slab of big, clever scientific thinking to the wider public. And while this is all very worthy, what I liked best about the trend was what we on *Focus* magazine called the 'infotainment stubby'. We coined the phrase in the editorial office to describe the fashionable pocket-sized 'biography of a thing' format that seemed to have a hot-line straight to Radio 4's *Book of the Week* and Channel 4's documentary producers.

The name itself came from the extremely ugly portmanteau word combining 'information' and 'entertainment' that was used a lot in the 1990s and which has now mercifully disappeared. The 'stubby' part came from the modest height of the book, little more that of a short bottle of beer, which our Australian sub-editor Keith Wilson called a 'stubby'. The daddy of the stubby was 4th Estate, and their crowning moments of glory were Dava Sobel's *Longitude*, David Ewing Duncan's *The Calendar* and, of course, Simon Singh's *Fermat's Last Theorem*. While we may all have enjoyed reading about the development of algebraic number theory in the 19th century, today probably few of us remember that the theorem itself stated that no three positive integers a, b, and c can satisfy the equation $a^n + b^n = c^n$ for any integer value of n greater than two.

What was so great about the infotainment stubby was that it was simply a moment of unashamed celebration of something fascinating. Over the years I collected many of these intriguing little volumes with subjects ranging from the giraffe to the coelacanth, from the compass to the passport, from the colour mauve to the vanilla pod, from solar eclipses to international cartographic theft, from the history of the *Oxford English Dictionary* to the relief of David Livingstone at Victoria Falls. I even started to write one myself about Cuban cigars and I've still got the rejection letters to prove it, including one from 4th Estate. Of course, they were not all published by 4th Estate, but it was this house that set the trend and it seemed obvious to me that there would one day be a collectors' market for the non-fiction stubby. Then I forgot about them … that is, until the postman handed me Helen Scales' *Poseidon's Steed*.

It always struck me that there were clear rules as to what made the stubby work. First, the subject had to be in some way related to popular science (Scales is a highly respected academic marine biologist). Second, the stubby needs to be a labour of love (again, Scales spent more than a decade scuba-diving around the world before she saw her first sea-horse in the wild, when she wanted to gaze at it 'forever, if I could'). Third, the research is required to uncover man-in-the-pub-style trivia. Here again Scales ticks the box, telling us that the human brain actually has two seahorses in it – the hippocampuses – that show signs of enlargement in London cabbies who've done 'the knowledge'. Fourth, the book should be small and easy to read (*Poseidon's Steed* has rather charmingly only six chapters); and finally the entire project has to teeter gracefully on the tightrope of irrele-vance. I think, with the greatest respect to Dr Scales' academic research, we can all agree that seahorses might just tick that box too. This last point is perhaps the most import-ant, because the infotainment stubby is above all a symbol of what publishers can achieve when they consult their imagination rather than their spreadsheets.

I decided to see for myself if the market for the stubby had started to develop, and as I trawled around the London book fairs last month I kept my eyes open, but didn't see anything to suggest my prediction had any merit. Maybe they're the wrong type of book for these fairs. Maybe insufficient time has passed for them to become scarce. Maybe these mass-market titles were just a flash-in-the pan (which should work in their favour as collectors' items). But then I saw something. On a stand at the ABA fair in Olympia I saw a very obscure title called *King Ink II* by the Australian musician, actor and writer Nick Cave. Not quite an authentic infotainment stubby, it does satisfy most of the conditions. It's small in stature, published in 1997, almost irrelevant, and an act of faith by the publisher. And while I accept that it is a book of pop song lyrics rather than a work of pop science, it is genuinely of its time and as an (albeit recent) literary archaeological artefact I thought it might provide some clues as to the condition of the 1990s non-fiction market. I was amazed to see that it was going for £795.

Also pleased. This is because in a past life as a music critic I had the dangerous pleasure of meeting Nick Cave on several occasions. In the late 1990s he was at his absolute zenith and, at the time of the *King Ink II* book-signing at Waterstone's in High Street Kensington in March 1997, the author of *And the Ass Saw the Angel* was in demand. As he signed my copy he was distracted by a photographer and inadvertently made his mark on both the title-page and the rear endpaper. *King Ink II* – so good he signed it twice.

As its name suggests, *King Ink II* is the follow-up to the original *King Ink* that was published in 1988. As sometimes happens, the sequel is considerably rarer than the first volume, which is understandable in a way because the publisher, cautious after seeing his hopes of glory dashed on the rocks of reality, reins in the print run for the successor.

Even so, I had trouble believing that the book in question was worth getting on for eight hundred quid and so I made enquiries in the trade. One insider came back to me saying that, although it was a little outside his field – let's face it, Nick Cave is a little outside everyone's field – he thought my copy might be worth £200 and that it was definitely worth collecting. If my source is right, this raises three interesting questions. First, what is it doing at a London book fair at a 400 per cent mark-up? Second, where are all the copies of *King Ink II*? And third, does this mean that it might now be time to start collecting early 4th Estate non-fiction? The answer to the first question is that *King Ink II* is possibly one of those books that hasn't yet got a 'settle down' value, while the answer to the second might well be 'charity shops, jumble sales and church bazaars'. But the answer to the third, in my book at least, is a resounding 'Yes. Grab them while you can.'

CHAPTER 27

Phases of the Moon

R ECENTLY I WAS asked to review the latest instalment
of Buzz Aldrin's autobiography – *Magnificent Desolation* – for an engineering magazine. Reasonable
enough: it's the 40th anniversary of the *Apollo 11* Lunar
Landing and, after all, 'Col Edwin E. Aldrin Jnr of the Air
Force', as the *New York Times* described him on 20th July
1969, was a test pilot, an astronaut and a man who could
compute orbital mechanics with a pencil on the back of
a cigarette packet. Although he descended the steps from
the Lunar Module *Eagle* a mere twenty minutes after Neil
Armstrong, who famously took the 'giant leap for Mankind',
Buzz was destined forever to be the second man on the
Moon. And you can bet that his time waiting to emerge
from the hatch was not spent in contemplation of the lines
from W.B. Yeats's 'Vacillation':

> And twenty minutes more or less
> It seemed, so great my happiness,
> That I was blessed and could bless…

The withering pathos of this extraterrestrial anticlimax is a note that sounds long and low in *Magnificent Desolation*, an account not so much of Aldrin's journey to the Moon, but his descent to hell upon his return. Unable to answer the question 'What next?' the all-American superhero slid into depression, unemployment and alcoholism. He became the world's most famous down-and-out and, as he says in his book, it's harder to be a bum when you're a celebrity than when you're no one. His grasp on reality at this point may have been limited, but it emerges he was sufficiently self-aware to know that he had to do something about his condition: his mother had committed suicide as a result of her depression and, frightened that the tendency might be inherited, Aldrin attended Alcoholics Anonymous meetings and became a national spokesman for the mentally ill.

Today we might regard it as a measure of the man that he could seek help, but in the 1970s the US military could not tolerate its heroes being anything other than perfect, and as a result Aldrin's career suffered terribly. Forced into early retirement, he ended up selling Cadillacs on a second-hand car lot to people who only wanted to shake the hand of an astronaut. His salvation came in the form of Lois Driggs Canon, the banking heiress he married on St Valentine's Day 1988. He's been a sober freelance astronaut ever since, advising governments and schoolchildren the world over on how to get back into space. In my review I rather enjoyed writing 'every Superman needs his Lois'. I meant well.

I wrapped up the review with: 'Buzz Aldrin's story is amazing, and *Magnificent Desolation* is inspirational.' Every word true and yet not everything I wanted to say. I attempted several qualifying variations on the theme of 'it's a shame that his book isn't as exciting as it should be, lacks psychological depth and adds nothing new to our understanding of *Apollo 11*,' but each time I hit the backspace key, telling myself that if I couldn't say something nice about Buzz's book I should keep my thoughts to myself.

Although it's hard to articulate precisely why, I think there may be two reasons for this. First: I like Buzz Aldrin and I don't want to hurt his feelings. Second: It's not his fault the book's a turkey. This is because *Magnificent Desolation* is one of those horrible things rushed out by an anniversary-obsessed publisher that has done no more than lazily commission a newspaper hack to siphon off a few of Buzz's better known opinions, slap it all down any-old-how between a set of boards and call it a book. That the UK publisher Bloomsbury was unwilling to send out advance proofs suggests (to me at least) they suspected *Magnificent Desolation* would not be reviewed well and that pre-publication publicity to that effect would almost certainly damage its high street sales. But that's Bloomsbury all over, who ever since they got lucky with the much-rejected J.K. Rowling have been far too big for their boots. Buzz's American publisher had no such stage fright or delusions of grandeur and I was able to pilfer a copy from a friend at the Explorers Club on a recent visit to New York.

I'm probably not alone in liking Aldrin, whose special appeal lies in such a colossus of a historic figure having such deeply tragic flaws. Despite these Shakespearian attributes, in person he comes across as a down-to-earth and hugely

161

likable man with more than a touch of razzamatazz. When you phone him at home his answering machine says, 'You've reached Lois and Buzz Aldrin,' and when he sends you an e-mail he signs off with a little graphic of an astronaut emblazoned with the words 'rocket hero'. Very few have earned the right to do that, and of those that have, only Buzz can get away with it. When I spoke to him recently his answer to my first question was, 'We have lift-off,' but that was only because my first question was, 'Are you ready?' I was about to start an interview with the great man and was checking the levels on my digital voice recorder.

From the perspective of human endeavour and exploration the *Apollo 11* Lunar Landing ranks among the great achievements of the 20th century. Social historians please note that for a merely important event to become a publicly owned global event something very odd needs to spontaneously happen. For no discernable reason the public has to share the desire to volunteer data about where they were when the event happened. What's interesting about this is that no one gives a damn where anyone was when these events unfolded and yet we insist, as with the Ancyent Marinere at the wedding reception, in stopping every third person and burdening them with our tale. For the record, when Neil Armstrong set foot on the Moon I was in bed. I know this because the time was 02:56 UTC and I wasn't allowed to stay up after Top of the Pops – *Apollo 11* or no *Apollo 11* – which seemed grossly unfair at the time, and still does.

For anyone interested, UTC or 'universal coordinated time' is a fancy version of Greenwich Mean Time. Please don't write in and say it isn't exactly, because I know that, but unless you're dealing with fractions of a second it amounts to roughly the same thing. Just in case you're wondering why the acronym doesn't follow the word order, you can blame that on the group of experts within the International Telecommunication Union that wanted to decide once and for all on a common acronym for the standard time that was used in technical applications such as international aviation, lunar landings and so on. Somewhat predictably the French reacted unhappily to the proposal that the acronym should follow the English word order. But an acronym following the French word order was equally unwelcome in the British camp. Since *Temps Universel Coordonné* gave the acronym TUC the Brits simply weren't having it. This was after all the decade of strikes, electricity shortages and piles of rotting rubbish on the street, and to some, 'Trades Union Congress' and acronyms based thereon were dirty words. Being scientists, the panel felt that the rational compromise was to arrange the letters in such a manner that the resulting acronym meant absolutely nothing to anyone. This hardly seems to have more than the slightest passing significance until you remember that these people are in charge of *time*.

Back in 1969, as Armstrong and Aldrin planted Old Glory on the Moon I was fast asleep. When I arrived at Parklands County Primary School the following morning, my teacher Miss Boyd was in a state of high excitement, telling us to hurry to the assembly hall. Once assembled, we sat cross-legged on the parquet floor watching a repeat of the broadcast on the school TV, while our headmaster 'Hitler' Jones

– complete with toothbrush moustache – paced up and down smoking a Woodbine, occasionally stopping to inform us that this was the greatest moment of our lives and that we'd remember it for ever.

Even now I recall the sense of occasion and how intently we watched those fuzzy black-and-white pictures. Talking to Buzz forty years on, the first thing that struck me was how intently he listens. He scans what you say in order to discover what he's really being asked, and having deciphered the code he locks on. Like an old-fashioned radio disc jockey he mentally reaches for the right jingle cartridge from the rack before slotting it into the jingle machine. We talk about the NASA Space Program, his depression and alcoholism. We talk about his life since he returned to earth and the future of space exploration. All too soon the allotted 45 minutes are nearing an end. And then, seemingly out of nowhere, he launched into a story that certainly wasn't known at the time and is hardly common knowledge today.

He told me that one of the first things he did after the Lunar Module (LM) *Eagle* landed on the surface of the Moon was to take communion. 'It was the right thing to do at the time,' he said, 'although we couldn't broadcast what I was doing, so I just asked people listening in to reflect upon what had been achieved.' The reason this part of the landing ritual was kept off air was because Madalyn Murray O'Hair, a prominent and litigious atheist, was in the process of suing NASA over the infamous *Apollo 8* Genesis reading, when astronauts William Anders, Jim Lovell, and Frank Borman took it in turns to recite the first ten verses of the

Old Testament while orbiting the Moon. O'Hair had argued that their actions were in violation of the First Amendment, and that since astronauts were government employees they were not allowed to perform such a broadcast. The Supreme Court had thrown the case out due to lack of jurisdiction, but NASA was understandably nervous and had put the block on any public religious activity during the *Apollo 11* mission.

Neil Armstrong's first words on the Moon had seriously deviated from the script and had caused alarm at Mission Control when he gave an improvised call signal as 'Tranquility base' and not 'Eagle'. During a lull in the transmission, Aldrin unpacked his communion kit, ate some space bread and drank a little vacuum-packed wine, something he kept secret for many years. As he uttered an oddly non-committal soliloquy there must have been some sweaty palms in Houston: 'This is the LM pilot. I'd like to take this opportunity to ask every person listening in, whoever and wherever they may be, to pause for a moment and contemplate the events of the past few hours and to give thanks in his or her own way.'

I said goodbye to Buzz thrilled to have spoken to one of my boyhood heroes and pleased that I'd finally engaged him on a subject he seemed genuinely happy to discuss. 'Are we done?' he said. I replied that we were and he told me that I should call on him time next time he came to 'jolly little England'. He's an engaging man with a lot to say. It's a shame his publisher has let him down so badly in allowing such a commercially cynical and poorly executed book to be released under his name.

Although my travels in pursuit of the Buzz Aldrin interview took me to New York – and subsequently to the launch of Mick Herron's novel Smoke and Whispers *in the Partners & Crime bookshop in the Village – what I remember most about the episode was writing this version of the article in a hotel lobby in Helsinki, where the barman repeatedly mistook me for someone by the name of Florian Schindler.*

CHAPTER 28

Breaking the ice
at the North Pole

F OR MORE THAN a decade I've been writing about
the North Pole: its exploration, climate, wildlife. And
although I've interviewed photographers, conserv-
ationists and sea captains, the people associated with the
Arctic that I've enjoyed listening to most are those writer-
explorers who have travelled in the region on foot. These
are the people who instinctively understand what it's like to
have ice in the blood, who write cracking tales of derring-
do. I've learned much about the region from classic explorers such as the late great Wally Herbert, as well as from
today's notables such as Pen Hadow. Over the years I've
become fascinated by what draws explorers to this icy desert
at the end of the earth and I've devoured their accounts of
hardship and starvation with a frisson of horror from the
comfort of the fireside. Not once did I ever expect I'd get
the chance to go to the frozen north myself.

Before the 20th century no one had even seen the North

167

Pole, much less set foot on it. We know that a century ago – in 1909 – US Naval Commander Robert E. Peary might have got there on foot with a team of dogs. He certainly believed he'd achieved his goal, but some commentators think he may have fallen short by as much as a hundred kilometers. Fergus Fleming, in his book *Ninety Degrees North*, describes the author of *Northward over the Great Ice* and *The North Pole* as 'undoubtedly the most driven, possibly the most successful and probably the most unpleasant man in the annals of polar exploration.' But did he get there? Wally Herbert, in his seminal *The Noose of Laurels*, says it simply wasn't possible to achieve all that Peary claimed in the time available. There were gaping holes in Peary's log and he didn't have proper navigational instruments with him, or a navigator.

Richard Byrd may or may not have reached ninety degrees north in an aeroplane in 1926. In 1948, Russian Alexandr Kuznetsov set off under the instructions of Joseph Stalin to fly north for scientific and strategic purposes, and in so doing became the first person to undisputedly set foot on the Pole. In 1968 Ralph Plaisted reached it from Canada by combination of snow scooter and air. In 1969 Briton Wally Herbert broke new ground, and his arrival at the North Pole by dog-sledge was the crowning moment of one of the great ice journeys of the 20th century.

Since these landmark expeditions, there have been many successful arrivals at the Pole by fixed-wing aircraft, helicopter and even parachute; by surface traverse, whether complete, one way or partial; by submarine (USS *Skate* was the first in 1959) or surface vessel. Of these, the first was the

Soviet icebreaker *Arktika* that reached the Pole on 17th August 1977. Since then there have been 65 Soviet or Russian voyages to the Pole, of which 64 have been in nuclear-powered ships. Twelve other icebreakers from five other nations have made token expeditions to the top of the world, but the Russians are the experts.

I joined the 50 Years of Victory – or the '50 лет Победы' – at Murmansk on the extreme northwest of Russia, on the Kola Bay. Way inside the Arctic Circle, the world's northernmost city consists almost entirely of glum communist tenements hastily thrown up after the Second World War. After near annihilation by the Germans, who had an airbase just eight minutes away, Murmansk was designated one of only twelve 'Hero cities' in Russia. In 1943, *Harper's* published an article about Murmansk by Dave Marlow called 'How it Looked to a Merchant Seaman', in which he quotes a Scots-Canadian mess-man: 'They've took a beating here.' The mosquitoes are like flying fortresses, and the only dabs of colour are the buttercups and dandelions that seem to grow everywhere in Murmansk.

We sailed for a week via Franz Josef Land, the northernmost Russian archipelago, and landed at Cape Tegetthof, where we saw the wind-blasted remains of explorers' huts. Then to Cape Fligley on Rudolf Island, from which Kuznetsov departed on his successful flight to the Pole. We saw polar bears, kittywakes, walruses, ivory gulls and memorials to dead explorers. But mostly I loafed around the Victory's library catching up on my polar reading.

'Library' might be too strong a word for the glass-fronted cabinets located perilously close a bizarrely inappropriate dartboard. These cabinets were stuffed with airport novels in an assortment of European languages. In amongst the dross were some extraordinary items of arctic literature, some of it quite rare, a lot of it justifiably forgotten, and without exception each volume in terrible condition. By the time we reached the higher latitudes we were crunching our way through the dense pack ice with hypnotic monotony. It provided the perfect background for putting the feet up and crunching through these seldom-read volumes: *Spring on an Arctic Island* by Katharine Scherman (Little, Brown, 1956), *Polar Exploration* by Andrew Croft (A. & C. Black, 1939), *Doctor's Wife in Greenland* by Inga Ehrström (George Allen & Unwin, 1955), *Land of the Pole Star* by Helge Ingstad (Jonathan Cape, 1966), *The Arctic Year* by Peter Freuchen and Finn Salomonsen (Putnam's 1958), *Clear Lands and Icy Seas* by Dorothea C. Stanwell-Fletcher (Dodd, Mead & Co, 1958), *The Trail of the Arctic Nomads* by Hugh Brandon-Cox (William Kimber, 1969), *Round About the North Pole* by W.J. Gordon (Dutton, 1907), *Where the Sea Breaks its Back,* by Corey Ford (Victor Gollancz, 1967), *Forty Thousand Against the Arctic,* by H.P. Smolka, (Hutchinson & Co, 1937) and *Return From the Pole,* by Frederick A. Cook (Burke, 1953).

When I eventually set foot on the ice at the North Pole I was the 22,500th person to do so, give or take a small margin for error created by the possibility of unrecorded military expeditions. I had with me my by now battered copy of *Ninety Degrees North* that Fleming had signed for me over a coffee in Victoria prior to my departure. Thinking that there can't be many copies of that particular book that had made it all the way to the Pole itself, I had the title-page imprinted with the ship's official passport-style stamp: 'The Geographic North Pole • 15 Juli 2009 • 90° N • 50 years of Victory'.

The Pole is, of course, an imaginary place, a point on a grid of invented geometry that in reality is no more or less impressive than a thin membrane of ice floating on the surface of the Arctic Ocean. The ice that is here today is not the ice that was here yesterday or will be here tomorrow. There is no marker other than one you may bring yourself – in our case a whacking great big red paddle – and the sapphire pools of water that lie on the surface of the multi-year ice are just as beautiful here as they were at eighty-nine degrees.

In his poem 'Burnt Norton' T.S. Eliot wrote of 'the still point of the turning world'. At the earth's 'axle-tree' he imagined the past and future to coalesce, a place where the spiritual and terrestrial worlds meet. Although it may be fanciful to say that to stand at the Pole is to stand with one foot in another world, if you look directly upwards along the earth's rotational axis you will come to Polaris, the North Star, the so-called celestial pole. Look down, and beneath your feet, after a couple of metres of sea ice, there are 4,000 metres of sea. Then, after 14,000 km of planetary mass, you will reach sea level at the South Pole, after which there are then another few hundred metres of rock, followed by 2,835 metres of ice. If you have maintained a straight line down through the globe you will end up almost in the middle of the geodesic dome of the Amundsen-Scott science research base at the South Pole. Don't expect a warm welcome: the people who work there are scientists and are notoriously hostile to visitors who are merely exploring.

The significance of the intersection of all lines of longitude depends as much on who you are and how you got there as anything else. I arrived at 11:57pm 15th July 2009 sitting in the bridge bar of the world's largest nuclear-powered icebreaker with a glass of ice-cold Russian vodka in my hand. Something like a hundred passengers from twenty-four countries had gathered below me on deck in the bright midnight sun to wander around with their global positioning systems, anxious to be the first to claim that theirs showed '90.00°N' exactly.

As champagne corks popped we cheered and congratulated each other on our passive achievement, as if we'd arrived on skis after weeks of doing battle with rubble fields, half-starved, frostbitten and with exhausted dogs. A ringed seal popped its head out of a channel of inky black water to see what the commotion was about, to find out what was breaking the rhythm of the creaking ice. Despite the kerfuffle, it was possible to detect something of the deep primal spirituality that has lured the great explorers of the past to what Pen Hadow once described as 'a pinprick of nothingness in the middle of nowhere'.

Accounts by explorers who arrive on foot after weeks of man-hauling sledges over pressure ridges vary wildly on how time at the Pole is spent. Some scrape together the last of their tobacco and alcohol for an all-too-brief party, while others become stranded, starving while they wait for the Twin Otter aeroplane to pick them up. Tom Avery, in his book *To the End of the Earth*, describes how in 2005 he arrived at the Pole with four other humans and sixteen dogs only to see an immaculately dressed woman step off a helicopter with a bottle of champagne. And he wasn't hallucinating: she was leading a small group of tourists who had flown to the Pole (presumably from an icebreaker) on a once-in-a-lifetime adventure holiday.

A century ago no one had been to the North Pole for certain. Today you can sail to ninety degrees north as a tourist on a Russian nuclear icebreaker. The jury will probably remain out forever on whether tourists should be allowed to travel to ecologically sensitive destinations such as the higher latitudes of the Polar Regions. But the prevailing sentiment on the 50 Years of Victory was that, provided the operator transacted its business responsibly, that the environment came first and that we didn't cause any unnecessary stress to the wildlife, then not only did we have a right to enter this pristine world, but we would come home as ambassadors, to write articles and tell our friends exactly what it is we're supposed to be protecting. I was glad that I'd set foot on the still point of the turning world, and glad too that I'd taken my copy of *Ninety Degrees North* with me. And in a roundabout way I was also pleased that somewhere along the voyage it had become intincted with red wine, rendering it worthless in financial terms. That, I thought, would at least guarantee that I never part with it.

CHAPTER 29

Notes from
a remote island

AS I WRITE, a ferry from mainland Sweden is gliding
past my hotel window in the yellow early evening
sun. It's on its way from Strömstad to the small
harbour of Ekenäs on the remote island of Solkoster, where
I'm reporting on the inauguration of Sweden's first marine
National Park for the *Daily Telegraph*. Lesser black-backed
and herring gulls are screaming on the stiff winds that whip
around the rocky islets and skerries of the Skagerrak and so
it's nice to be indoors, even though it's not obvious what I'm
going to write in my article.

Civic obsequies are tedious at best, but when conducted
in a language beyond even the faintest understanding they
can be excruciating. This is a shame because the master of
ceremonies is the environmentalist and writer Stefan
Edman, Sweden's David Attenborough, if you like. One of
the local fishermen – Anders – speaks almost perfect
English and so I ask him to translate for me. Edman, it

seems, has been charged with introducing a *smörgåsbord* of council flunkies, minor celebrities and locals-who-can't-be-left-out. They're all in a state of hyperventilation because the King of Sweden is arriving at any minute by helicopter to ring the bell that will mark the opening of the National Park.

Anders tells me they're talking a load of puffed-up nonsense, but one dignitary in particular has taken matters a step too far in delivering a speech outlining his trepidation and joy at the successful production and delivery of his speech. According to Anders, he's full of warm thoughts about himself, the quality of his oration and the impression his rhetoric will no doubt make on the King when he comes to hear of it. Anders is by contrast a no-nonsense person, with the sort of straight talk I admire, and so as I rush back to my hotel composing the headline 'King rings in new era for Scandinavian ecology', I'm also just as concerned that this month's 'Double Booked' doesn't become a column about a column.

Sweden's windswept strands all seem a million miles away from a rather slick evening at Bafta house I attended the week before, where Alexander McCall Smith was launching his latest novel – *Corduroy Mansions* – before a crowd of invited *Telegraph* readers. It was one of those rainy London evenings when everybody seems to bump into you, blow smoke at you or get on your nerves. Even the majestic No 9 Routemaster double-decker bus that plies its trade in the West End, instead of drawing gasps of admiration merely splashes the passer-by. I'd seen *Corduroy Mansions* advertised on huge posters on the Underground, and had managed to snaffle a ticket for the *Telegraph* reader event on the rather flimsy basis that as a *Telegraph* writer I was pretty much entitled to one.

Of course, I was unfashionably on time for the event and so, not wishing to be the first to arrive, I decided to shelter from the rain in Hatchards a few doors down Piccadilly. Keen readers of 'Double Booked' will know that I've not always shown much in the way of goodwill towards Hatchards and so for me to use the establishment for my own convenience is a rank hypocrisy for which I apologise. As I browsed the sweet-smelling new books I felt like one of those serial murderers that can't quite resist the temptation to return to the scene of the crime. Consumed by guilt I unbuckled the purse and parted with sufficient coin of the realm to separate Hatchards from a paperback copy of Justin Marozzi's *The Man Who Invented History*, Seamus Heaney's new translation of *The Testament of Cresseid* and Ronald Blythe's *The Bookman's Tale*, which I'll come back to later.

Corduroy Mansions is a milestone in the process of what marketers call 'product delivery'. Following his success in publishing the '44 Scotland Street' novels in daily fascicles in the *Scotsman* newspaper, McCall Smith has now written the first proper online novel, appearing in instalments on the *Telegraph* website. Of course, there are countless novelists and publishers out there that have posted their work online, and there are even more 'outsider' artists for whom cyberspace is the publishing equivalent of the Elysian Fields, but this is the first time an author of McCall Smith's status has taken on such an enterprise.

At Bafta, McCall Smith's guests drank warm chardonnay and bought copies of the bound-up version of the online novel for him to sign. These were being offered at a whopping discount and the wine was free, a rare example of a publisher – in this case the worthy Polygon – doing the decent thing and treating their punters with respect bordering on kindness. Ever jolly, McCall Smith inscribed his books, shared jokes with his admirers and, the highlight of the evening, read a few snippets from the as yet unnamed sequel to *Corduroy Mansions*.

One of these extracts was a charming and extremely funny piece about Cecil Court, which we all know and love as one of the finest streets in London – or anywhere else for that matter – for browsing antiquarian bookshops. This is something that may have been lost on McCall Smith's character, who seemed more intent on buying a Buddhist or Tibetan – I can't remember exactly which – hat. The successful hat, it transpires, came neither from Tibet nor anywhere else remotely connected with Buddhism, and neither was it made by a Tibetan person, or even a Buddhist. But it did externally resemble a Buddhist or Tibetan hat in that it had been knitted (by an obliging woman in, I think, Pimlico), which satisfied in McCall Smith's character what was required of the object in question. Pressing his point home, McCall Smith observed that those of a more precise inclination would prefer the soul of the hat to be as authentic as possible, while regarding its outward appearance as immaterial. The audience was in fits and everyone left happy – despite the rain – clutching their signed *Corduroy Mansions*.

Which, despite its gentle humour, is a book of the computer age. Originally published in the digital domain, it was also written using digital technology. I know this because I once visited McCall Smith at his Edinburgh home, and as you are shown into his writing room the first thing you see is an enormous iMac on his leather-topped desk. Nothing unusual in that, you might think, but there are still writers – Ronald Blythe among them – yet to embrace the digital age, preferring their original manual typewriters or even a fountain pen. Now in his late eighties, the spritely Blythe writes of his dislike of 'computerish' prose. Quite what he'd make of *Corduroy Mansions* I do not know, although I suspect that, through their shared love of W.H. Auden, he and McCall Smith would get along famously. It's hard not to admire a poet that would work religiously every day until cocktail time, if only on the *Telegraph* crossword.

Blyth's latest – *The Bookman's Tale* – is one of those books that simply can't be praised highly enough. How can a man know so much, be so wise, have such generosity of spirit and write so beautifully? This slender book is the sixth in a series of anthologies of his Wormingford column in the *Church Times*. In some respects these pieces are the definition of what a good column should be. More a conversation with his readers, or one half of an old-fashioned correspondence, the columns were intended to comment on matters arising in the church year. But Blythe is such a fine pastoral writer that inevitably the liturgical calendar becomes blended with the passing of the seasons, the planting and harvesting of crops, the pollarding of trees, the setting out of badger nets.

On top of this, Blythe can never resist sharing what he's reading, and what literary chums he's had around for tea and cake both literally and metaphorically. His ancient farmhouse is a bucolic haven where writers, painters and composers gather to gossip.

There is so much good stuff in Blythe's columns – material I feel instinctively familiar with – that my immediate reaction is one of fear that I'll end up copying them. 'I wish I'd said that,' an admirer supposedly said to Oscar Wilde. 'You will,' said Wilde apocryphally. But just to make sure that I never – even subconsciously – claim them for myself, here are some of Blythe's best bits – and he's not often better than when he's telling a joke. Let's start with an impossibly silly literary anecdote, almost certainly untrue and definitely the better for it. Blythe likes this story so much, and has told it so many times, that he can't remember if it's found its way into a Wormingford column before. But it doesn't matter. The story goes that Alexandre Dumas once bounded into his kitchen in a heightened state of agitation. 'My dear,' he's supposed to have announced to his wife, 'at last I have finished writing *The Three Musketeers*.' To which the good Madame Dumas replied somewhat non-sequiturishly: 'But there is still an hour until dinner.' With which the crestfallen Dumas promptly returned to his desk to start *The Black Tulip*. Did you hear the one about the aborigine who bought himself a new boomerang, asks Blythe, informing us that it is yet another one of his favourite jokes. He couldn't get rid of the old one.

Of course, the Wormingford column is also very serious indeed. Blythe writes of comforting dying friends, of funerals, of becoming old; of death, immortality and how to live properly. He writes of Maytime and larks, apples and bread, the old saints and ploughing; John Clare and George Herbert, Wilfred Owen and Charles Causley. He laments the passing of the old ways of the country, the tailing off of the congregation, loud televisions. Blythe writes in beautiful, almost celestial prose of such delicacy that the ink barely touches the paper. Perhaps this is to be expected from a man who wrote the classic *Akenfield*, once described as 'the best portrait of modern rural life in England', and which John Updike thought 'exquisite'.

Meanwhile, back in Sweden, I snap shut my copy of *The Bookman's Tale*, wishing it were a thousand pages longer, and prepare for the long slog back to Blighty. There's only one book left in my luggage that I've not read and that's Stefan Edman's *Koster Sea*, an illustrated coffee-table book about the marine ecology of the west coast of Sweden, a bit like David Attenborough's *Life on Earth*, if you like. I flick through it, admiring some extremely accomplished underwater photography, noticing that the copy I'd been given was signed by the author. I'm just about to put it back in my bag when I notice that Edman has included a quotation from Ebba Lindqvist's 'Sommar och vinter', a marvellous poem from her important collection *Fiskeläge* ('Fishing Village') that describes the changing of the seasons in the Swedish islands:

> And this is summer:
> Fresh mackerel, fresh mackerel!
> Morning, lunch and supper
> And this is winter:

Salt mackerel, salt mackerel!
Morning, lunch and supper

I can't help feeling some sympathy for the fishermen of the Skagerrak and their unvaried lives, catching and eating mackerel. They must have been bored to tears in their salty paradise. And today as I leave their world behind, as is so often the case, the journey home seems much longer than the outbound leg. Sitting in the departure lounge in Gothenburg, the city where Lindqvist grew up, with hundreds of angry people waiting to board a plane that's now two hours late, I know that I've missed this evening's private view of Nick Danziger's *Between Heaven and Earth: a Journey through Christian Ethiopia*. And once again I say that's that, I'm never going away again.

The sequel to Corduroy Mansions *was eventually entitled* The Dog who Came in from the Cold.

In 2000 Stephen King started to publish his novel The Plant *online in instalments, a project that would have made him the first major novelist to write a book this way. The project is yet to be completed.*

CHAPTER 30

In search of southern Spain

ERHAPS IT'S a sign that I have too much spare time but, thinking I'd discovered a typo in a recent edition of T.S. Eliot's *Collected Poems 1909-62*, I started prowling around the house, muttering under my breath, looking for my set of first edition pamphlets of 'Four Quartets'. Emboldened by a rather blatant bottle of 1996 Faustino Rioja *gran reserva*, I set off to prove that a rogue comma had jumped ship and had skewed the theosophical axis of Eliot's greatest poem.

After what seemed like several hours of moving boxes and peering with a torch into the rows of books behind rows of books, I eventually found what I was looking for, along with an unexpected bonus. Here was a long-neglected A4 plastic sleeve containing not four, but five Faber & Faber pamphlets, with their unmistakable air of austerity and sobriety. Four were of course the Quartets and it was the work of a minute to discover that the comma in question had always been where the worthy editors, typesetters and compositors at Faber had originally put it. The fifth was a misfiled dusty rose-coloured volume by W.H. Auden, slightly sunned and a little creased at the corners, called simply 'Spain'.

These old Faber pamphlets are wonderful things, with their matte dust-wrappers confidently overprinted in bold black lettering, their interior pages yellowing and staples rusting. Along with the contemporary designs of the Hogarth Press covers, they tell of a heyday of great British men of letters whose responsibility was to help a nation through the dark times of economic depression followed by global warfare. And good value they were too: my copy of 'Spain', published in May 1937 (renamed 'Spain 1937' in later editions), cost one shilling ('All the author's royalties from the sale of this poem go to *Medical Aid for Spain*'). At some point I'd paid £45 for it, which seems about right, although there are plenty of booksellers – particularly in the United States – that think that it's worth more than a hundred pounds. Given that you can still get signed firsts of Auden and MacNeice's *Letters From Iceland* for that, this seems to be highly unlikely.

'Spain' is an important poem and definitely worth collecting, despite Auden later refusing to include it in collections of his poetry. He'd apparently disowned it on the basis that the political standpoint it explored wasn't his, but a literary construct with which to make a narrative point. Absolute piffle, of course – he'd made a mistake and he knew it. We can agree on just how feeble this argument can sometimes be – virtually every magazine in the dentist's waiting room will contain somewhere variations on the theme of 'the opinions expressed in this publication are not necessarily the views of the publisher or the editor'. It always amazes me that anyone could seriously think that printing this tagline would prevent a court appearance if one of their contributors had libelled someone.

But Auden was clearly embarrassed about what he had written, I think, and rather than make too many excuses he did the decent thing and simply removed it from the canon. Caught up in the romance and rhetoric of the Spanish Civil War, he wrote of the 'conscious acceptance of guilt in the necessary murder'. This is probably no more than a fancy way of saying 'a man's got to do what a man's got to do', but it sits oddly with his High Anglicanism and it is hardly surprising he regretted using the expression. George Orwell made things worse for Auden when he criticised 'Spain' in his book of essays *Inside the Whale*: 'It so happens that I have seen the bodies of numbers of murdered men – I don't mean killed in battle, I mean murdered. Therefore I have some conception of what murder means – the terror, the hatred, the howling relatives, the post-mortems, the blood, the smells. To me murder is something to be avoided.'

It was largely because he'd had enough of the grand-scale industrialised murder of the trenches of the Western Front during the Great War that the young author and essayist Gerald Brenan made his way to Southern Spain in 1919. Having seen active service at Ypres and on the Somme, he yearned for a period of freedom in his life, and so, armed only with savings from his war service pay and a great many books, he set off to give himself the education the Great War had denied him. He eventually settled in the tiny, isolated village of Yegen deep in the dramatic and stunning Alpujarras mountain range that stretches south from the Sierra Nevada. His experiences in this primitive region, where he remained for several years, playing host to members of the Bloomsbury Group, are the basis of perhaps one of the best books about Spain – *South From Granada*.

There are of course plenty of good books on the Iberian peninsular – Jan Morris's *The Presence of Spain* and George Borrow's *The Bible in Spain* among them – but *South From Granada* for me is the keystone of any serious collection on the subject. Writing in the self-consciously literary prose of the Edwardian withdrawing room, Brenan alternates lengthy descriptions of his personal experiences in the mountains with lecture-style chapters about the geology, religion, economy and social conventions of the region. Although it informs more than it entertains, and as such might be tiresome to the modern reader used to television documentaries, *South From Granada* benefits from its tweedy, pipe-smoking, cricket-playing geniality of a bygone age. There are times – as in his chapter on the brothels of the south coast – when Brenan enjoys the disparity between style and content, and the results are often hilarious.

Although my UK first edition of *South From Granada* has a superb duotone cover illustration of Andalusian rural architecture by Patricia Davey, this isn't the best image to have found its way onto the cover of this wonderful Spanish travelogue. That honour goes to Augustus John's magnificent painting *Mulhacén* that graces the Penguin Travel Library paperback edition from the late 1990s. Named after one of the Muslim kings of Granada, the

stately Mulhacén is the highest peak on the Iberian peninsular, much loved by John, who painted it while visiting
Brenan.

Following in both men's footsteps, I've walked through
this part of the Alpujarras on several occasions, terrified by
the precipitous mountain roads. In something of a baptism
of fire, on the first evening of my first visit my guide led me
from the village of Bubión to Capileira and beyond. We
ambled in the late evening sun along an almost forgotten
ancient trail – one of the highest in Europe – to a small
wooden shack where we drank bottled beer and listened to
what I was told was *real* flamenco guitar music. Men and
women with heavy clogs performed traditional flamenco
dancing without a castanet or a maraca in sight. As the
evening wore on the sky became black, the mountain air
became cold and we could see the flickering campfires of
the gypsies that were supposed to live deep in the forest.
My guide had disappeared and, as I fumbled my way back
down the mountain by moonlight, the only other living
souls I saw were a man, dead drunk, asleep on his horse
mildly ambling home.

The following day dawned and I decided to try to find
the vantage point from which John had painted Mulhacén.
I'd heard that one of the best walks was across country to
Trevelez, at the head of a valley on the road to Yegen and
famous for its Jamón Serrano (or 'mountain ham'). After
twenty miles of hard slog over rough ground I finally arrived
at Trevelez, where I found a small bookshop that seemed to
sell only copies of Chris Stewart's *Driving Over Lemons*, the
former Genesis drummer's autobiographical sketches of his

life as an exile in the Alpujarras. Poking around, I managed to find a few copies of *South From Granada*, as well as an intriguing little book by Gamel Woolsey called *Death's Other Kingdom*, a slim memoir of the Spanish Civil War. Realising that I wasn't going to make the return journey on foot before nightfall, I walked into a local bar and ordered the coldest beer in the house and a local minicab to take me back to Bubión. The taxi ride home took a depressingly swift twenty minutes.

There's no evidence that there were taxis in the Alpujarras in Brenan's time – Roman Catholicism didn't even reach this remote outpost of Spain until the 20th century – but we do know that Brenan had a habit of taking them while in London. In a story I heard from a friend of a friend of Brenan's great-nephew, I learned that even at a great age Brenan was still 'a libidinous fellow'. The story goes that he would often take a taxi going up Piccadilly and, upon spying a toothsome young secretary or two out for their lunchtime stroll, he'd roll down the window and ask the young ladies to lunch. In one of the unkindest moments in literary gossip, no one seems to know the outcome of such moments, but I'm prepared to put money on Edward Fitzgerald Brenan – or Don Geraldo as he was known by the good folk of Yegen – being successful from time to time.

Quite what Gamel Woolsey would have made of all this is not entirely clear but, given that she was Brenan's wife, it's probable that she'd have disapproved. Although primarily a poet, Woolsey's *Death's Other Kingdom* is perhaps her best-known book today, in part due to its reissue by Eland. Slender, poetic and moving, it's an account of how her idyllic existence in the Andalusian village of Malaga dis-integrated as the Spanish Civil War consumed all in its wake. In her quite extraordinarily lyrical prose, she describes how she turned her home from an artistic enclave into a sanctuary for the petrified locals while her husband (who'd seen it all before) set about writing books on Spanish history. Woolsey is less composed, however, and undergoes a transformation as startling as the destruction of her beloved landscape. Her diaphanous exterior deteriorates as she obsesses over protecting the local peasantry, who are faced with the ever-increasing possibility of a violent end.

First editions of *Death's Other Kingdom* are not common, although you occasionally see them in pretty poor condition for about £50. A much better bet is her first book, a col-lection of poems called *Middle Earth*, but steer clear of her novel *One Way of Love*, that had been due for publication in 1930 but was spiked because of its alleged sexual explicit-ness. Virago eventually brought out an edition in 1987, and you may be assured it's every bit as unenticing as the dull olive green livery of the publishing house that brought it into this world.

The reason *Death's Other Kingdom* keeps popping in and out of print is almost certainly that Spanish Civil War memoirs by US women poets don't have much of a market. That may be so, but within these admittedly narrow para-meters this is a very important book, offering a brilliantly rendered perspective on a moment in history that has achieved iconic status. My only nagging doubt about *Death's Other Kingdom* is from where Woolsey might have dredged the title up. Of course, there's the line in T.S. Eliot's 'The

Hollow Men' – 'Is it like this/In death's other kingdom' – but my suspicion is that the phrase has far deeper roots, and I can't quite bring myself to believe that an early-20th-century poem, no matter how important, can sustain the weight of titlehood for another poet's memoirs, even a fellow American's. But, try as I might, I can't find the expression anywhere in Shakespeare or even in the Bible. Which makes me think, if Eliot didn't pinch the line from either of these, then where the hell did he pinch it from?

CHAPTER 31

The road
from Damascus

I DON'T SUPPOSE it will ever be possible to work out whether two millennia ago the convention of naming streets was still in its infancy, or if the people who wrote the Bible simply weren't interested in thoroughfare nomenclature. But in the entire biblical canon there is only one road mentioned by name. And it's not as you might think the road to Damascus, but a road *in* Damascus, one also forever connected with the conversion of St Paul.

In the Acts of the Apostles the disciple Ananias has a vision of God in which he is told to 'go into the street which is called Straight, and enquire in the house of Judas for one called Saul, of Tarsus.' Ananias goes to the house and lays his hands on Saul, a one-time persecutor of Christians. The scales fall from Saul's eyes and the rest is history. I visited St Ananias Chapel on a recent visit to Syria, the very place where St Paul is thought to have been baptised. But it's best not to get too excited by this – there are several sites pressing the same claim. Still, it's nice to enjoy the ambience of the underground chapel that was once at street level but has slowly been buried under of thousands of years of archaeological detritus.

The Street Called Straight – or the *Via Recta* as the Romans called it – runs from west to east through the old town of Damascus, from the Suq El-Kumeleh to Bab Charki, or the Gate of the Sun, where it divides the Christian and the Jewish Quarters. It's atmospheric not only for its religious associations – there are mosques and churches on every corner – but for its smart bustling air of fashionable metropolitanism. Apart from being the place where pilgrims, travellers and the curious congregate to start exploring this exhilarating city, this is also where trendy young Damascenes meet to drink coffee, discuss the affairs of the day and play backgammon.

If this all sounds slightly familiar it might be because so little has changed since travel writer Colin Thubron described the world's oldest city in his *Mirror to Damascus*. As well as heralding the start of a glittering career, Thubron's first book remains one of the few in modern times devoted to this great Syrian city. While Freya Stark, Gertrude Bell, Esther Stanhope and a whole host of letter and journal writers going back to Ibn Battutah and beyond have revelled in the haunting landscapes of this little-travelled part of the Levant, no one it seems – apart from Thubron – thought it worth close and exclusive treatment.

But Thubron was right to see something special in Syria. The attraction is, of course, its unbroken history: while in Egypt or Greece you can travel to the great sites of antiquity and ponder on what life might have been like, in Damascus you can walk down the back streets of the Bible. Thubron went one better and lived in the Street Called Straight with a poor Arab family. While staying with them he visited many of the city's thousands of mosques, attended the public baths, witnessed dervish dances and almost found the head of John the Baptist.

Reading *Mirror to Damascus* in the courtyard of the sumptuous Shahbandar Palace Hotel, what strikes me as most remarkable is simply how good Thubron's debut was. Even allowing for his being a hardened TV journalist by the time he came to write it, there can be very few first outings as well written and as authentic as this. Those familiar with Thubron's more recent *Shadow of the Silk Road* will recognise the deeply poetic contemplations, intricacy of expression and self-consciously literary approach to his subject. While others unicycle around the Pyramids at Giza, or drag a fridge around Ireland, Thubron pays homage to the great writers from the backwaters of history while hardly giving a fig for the transitory conventions of modernity. It comes as no surprise to discover that he's descended from the great Restoration poet John Dryden.

Published in 1967 by Heinemann, my copy of *Mirror to Damascus* is a first edition that Thubron signed for me a few years ago when I visited his home in West London to interview him for a travel magazine. The cover is the author's own rather grainy photograph of the Tekkiye Mosque in Damascus, with the book's title set in a typeface that hasn't been seen a great deal since the mid-1970s. While the silver-haired writer clanked around in his kitchen making coffee and cursing the persistent failure of the London Underground, I sat in his reading room browsing a library divided equally between the modern English novel and 20th-century travel literature. I made mental notes about the piles of review books that had been sent to him by publishers and friends in the hope of a friendly reaction, while thoroughly approving of a gigantic stuffed bird of prey – which I'm pretty sure was a Eurasian eagle owl, *Bubo bubo* – that he'd smuggled back from Spain 'in the days when you could do that sort of thing.'

Although Damascus is Syria's main attraction, there's so much more for the bookworm than the country's capital. The guidebooks tell you to expect masses of Islamic and Christian devotional architecture, crusader citadels and Roman ruins, and you're hardly disappointed. But there's also a slightly faded colonial atmosphere to some of the dusty cities outside Damascus. This is never more apparent than in the old town in Aleppo, where you can drink in a fabulous bar where T.E. Lawrence famously left an unpaid bill. With its ancient leather club chairs, Bakelite ashtrays and threadbare Turkish carpets, nothing at Baron's Hotel seems to have changed since the war. I met an old travelling companion here for a nightcap and as we drank glass after glass of Johnnie Walker whisky, smoking caporal cigarettes, we wondered what great travellers had done the very same in this very bar.

As the hour wore on, a procession of literary ghosts began to take their places for the night and it became obvious why this time capsule of a hotel is such a magnet for explorer-types who've lost their way in Aleppo. Agatha Christie stayed here – in fact she wrote *Murder on the Orient Express* at Baron's – while travelling to join her husband archaeologist Sir Max Mallowan at Palmyra. At the National Museum in Aleppo just around the corner there's a selection of artefacts recovered by Mallowan, including part of a golden frieze – as well as stone rosettes, idols and amulets – from the altar of the Temple of the Eye. Something of an Indiana Jones of his day, Sir Max was much appreciated by Agatha, who is supposed to have remarked, with her incisive logic, on how fortunate she was to be married to an archaeologist. The older you get, said Agatha, the more interest he shows.

While I can't speak for Gertrude Bell, Freya Stark or any of the other early lady travellers I admire so much, I do know that the historian and travel writer William Dalrymple passed through Aleppo. In *From the Holy Mountain* he writes: 'I sat at the brow of the hill munching the sandwiches they had packed for me at the Baron, looking down over the extraordinary expanse of late antique buildings spread out across the valley below.' Dalrymple was on his way from Aleppo to the Church of St Simeon Stylites, the early Christian aesthete who, in an attempt to rid himself of the attentions of the material world, sat on top of an eighteen-metre pillar for thirty-seven years. Although very little is known about the saint, Marius Kociejowski has managed to piece together as much detail as he can from the three contemporary Lives of Simeon in *The Street Philosopher and the Holy Fool*, before reaching the conclusion: 'The man disturbs as much as he inspires.'

An old-fashioned cassette recorder plays the muffled bars of a forgotten Big Band, while tarnished brass fans rotate elegantly, slowly pulling the cracked plaster from the high ceiling. For a moment, through the cigarette smoke, I can see Lawrence of Arabia pushing aside his campaign maps, picking up his fountain pen and writing 'another letter from this beautiful hotel, whose face you must be getting to know by heart'. At Baron's there's a small cabinet of Lawrence memorabilia, including, of course, the unpaid bill.

Aleppo. So good that Shakespeare – or *Shaykh-al-Spear*, as I am told the Bard is in Arabic – mentions it twice. There is an appearance in *Macbeth*, but far more dramatic is the reference in *Othello*, where the Moor of Venice shows off his knowledge of Middle Eastern geography while in the act of stabbing himself to death:

> ... Set you down this;
> And say besides, that in Aleppo once,
> Where a malignant and a turban'd Turk
> Beat a Venetian and traduced the state,
> I took by the throat the circumcised dog,
> And smote him, thus.

And thusly smote, we drifted downstream along the river Euphrates, that with the Tigris defines Mesopotamia and sculpts the shape of modern Iraq. Flowing down from the Taurus Mountains in Turkey, the river's name derives from the Greek meaning 'fruitful'. And as we turn from the vineyards and orchards of its banks we move south into the desert for another mighty ruin with literary connections.

195

In Palmyra I unpack again at the Zenobia hotel where Dame Agatha stayed during one of her many peregrinations in the Levant. For those interested, the Queen of Crime's room today is totally featureless and would hardly be worth a second glance were it not for the truly stunning view she had, straight over this ancient caravan city, the so-called bride of the desert. Partially restored, Palmyra has an apocalyptic 'cities in dust' atmosphere that only increases as you wander through its broken stones at night. A UNESCO World Heritage Site, it's probably unique in that you can walk among the ruins unhindered. There are no fences, guards or 'keep out' signs – only the long shadows of the tower tombs and arcades of pillars in the dusty desert sunset. I can imagine the archaeologist's wife sitting at the window patiently waiting for her husband to return from the dig, writing her oriental mysteries that were once so glamorous. Her patience is famous – she became a dab hand at reconstructing entire amphorae from random shards of ceramic.

Palmyra is a wonderful place to wander around by day, but it's magical to stroll among these toppled ruins by moonlight. As the warm desert wind whips around the majestic tetrapylon, it's easy to see how Palmyra could inspire monumental poetry. Shelley would have blown a gasket at the sight of these mighty works, and the 'lone and level sands'. And while boring academics waste their time debating the exact geographical location of Browning's 'Love Among the Ruins' – with all its burning blood and palpitating erotic grandeur – I'll give you any odds you like it was written with Palmyra very much in mind.

All too soon it's time to return to Damascus, back to the Street Called Straight, the rooftop restaurants and the atmospheric late-night bars. I decide to pay a final visit to the House of Saint Ananias, but on my way a man stops me on Hananiya Street and invites me into his trinket shop. A devout Christian, he tells me he once played the part of Paul in a movie version of the saint's life. We drink glasses of sweet tea and he tells me his story, listing the places I should visit if I have any time left over – the Armenian Church, the Jewish Quarter, the shrine of Saint George. As we say goodbye, I look ruefully at the 'traditional Damascene dagger' he sold me, and wonder how much of his story is true. Wandering back to the Shambandar Palace for the last time, walking through these ancient convoluted streets, it's time to take my leave of Thubron's city of the imagination, a wonderfully resonant city that seems to have so much more atmosphere than rainy, bloody London.

CHAPTER 32

Friendship in
the wooden world

F ROM TIME TO time all Londoners must think of the
metropolis as wet, grey and boring, but in January
2000, as I prepared to board a British Airways flight
to Nairobi, it was beyond dull and the worst city in the world
bar none. As I climbed the wet aircraft staircase, clutching
a copy of the *Daily Telegraph* to my chest, I'd never been
quite so anxious to get out of Blighty. Once again I'd been
relieved of the editor's chair at a swanky Soho magazine
office, and once again I'd suffered a concocted 'redundancy'
at the hand of an idiot publisher who did management
speak with a chavy estuary twang. We all have times when
we say 'never again', only this time I was going to say it from
the idyll of a white coral strand spang in the middle of the
Indian Ocean.

It must have been a slow news day because the story
above the fold was the death of the novelist Patrick O'Brian.
You don't often see writers making front-page headlines and

the last time I recall anything similar was Graham Greene's death in 1991. I could understand all the fuss about Greene – he's one of our greatest novelists – but Patrick O'Brian at the time was for me little more than a modern C.S. Forester, with a reputation for being almost impossible to read. And while the *Times* might well have called him 'the greatest historical novelist of our time' I'd never had the inclination to discover what the commotion was all about.

As I changed planes and boarded a rickety old De Havilland Dash-7 bound for Zanzibar, I picked up another copy of the *Telegraph*, this time with an obituary on O'Brian of a length normally reserved for important military generals or theoretical physicists. By the time I'd cleared customs, the inescapable truth was that a literary behemoth had eluded me. By the time I was wandering the narrow streets of Stone Town, where the old spice traders' houses are now backpackers' hostels, I realised that I couldn't care less, and so dived into the Africa House Hotel for a sundowner.

After a few days' sailing around the islands off the west coast of Zanzibar, I hired a local guide to drive me to the other side of the island, where I thought I'd drop anchor for a week or two. No one actually needs a driver in Zanzibar, but as Mr Ali charged only a few dollars and there were military checkpoints to negotiate and he had a permit, it was all so much easier that way. 'Where are you going?' asked Mr Ali, a rather westernised liberal Muslim who enjoyed beer and cigarettes for lunch. I told him that I wasn't sure, but as long as we got there before dark I'd be perfectly happy.

And so I was. By nightfall I was established in a beach hut in Jambiani costing US$5 a night, which I shared with a family of rather vocal ducks. As I sat on a wall in the village, I watched long silver fish leap elegantly out of the green sea in the twilight. A man approached me and told me his name was Captain and offered to take me fishing the following day if I was interested. And so the days rolled by, sailing out past the women seaweed farmers in the lagoon, out to the reef where we caught white fish on hand-lines with what Captain called 'material of octopus' for bait. In the evenings I fried some of the fish and ate it with sticky rice and mango. Captain taught me the rudiments of Swahili, and whenever I became frustrated with my lack of linguistic facility I listened to Led Zeppelin tapes in the local Oyster Hotel bar.

The trouble with Paradise is that it's bloody boring and before long there came a day when I simply had to get something decent to read. I telephoned Mr Ali and told him my sorrows. 'Stay there,' he encouraged me. 'I'll come to pick you up and I'll take you to the best bookshop on the island.' A few hours later Mr Ali turned up in Jambiani in his bright red Mini Moke, tooting and smiling and waving a cigarette about. And a few hours after that I was back in Stone Town in a boutique called the Zanzibar Gallery. It was a bookshop of sorts, where it seemed you could buy any book you liked so long as you wanted nothing more than a biography of Frederick Courteney Selous – *The Mighty Nimrod* by Stephen Taylor – or one of a mass of seemingly identical HarperCollins paperbacks by Patrick O'Brian. To this day I have no idea why, I picked up a sunned and cracking copy of *The Ionian Mission* at random, disbursed the US $20 and spent the rest of the day visiting the stupendous Anglican

Cathedral deep in the heart of Stone Town. Built on the site of the old slave market in the late 1800s, its altar is said to mark the spot of the original whipping post where slaves were tied and beaten, to show off their stamina and quality to potential buyers. Nearby there's a monument where the statues of a family have been erected in a deep pit, their necks joined by an original slave chain from mainland Africa. There is also a crucifix made from the tree beneath which Dr Livingstone's heart was buried at Chitambo, where he died.

The road back to Jambiani was fraught with drama. As we drove through Jozani forest I heard a nasty clunk, as if the gearbox had struck something hard. It had. A Zanzibar Red Colobus (*Piliocolobus kirkii*) that was now lying on the road in terminal agony. We stopped to see what could be done, and that was how I killed my first monkey. We continued our journey in silence and when we reached Jambiani I said goodbye to Mr Ali.

It was several days later when I finally got around to opening *The Ionian Mission*. Within minutes I realised I was reading something quite special and immediately began to regret not buying more volumes while I had the chance. I remembered that the *Telegraph* journalist had been mildly baffled as to how an author as difficult as O'Brian could be so popular. Truth is I didn't find him difficult at all, once I'd worked out my spankers from my topgallants. And even when I couldn't disentangle my barques from my brigantines, or my corvettes from my corsairs, I enjoyed the poetry of the jargon of the Great Age of Sail, rolling along to the rhythms of the storms and swells. I also liked it that *The*

Ionian Mission was so obviously about male friendship in the controlled, confined space of the 'wooden world', reminiscent of Jane Austen's examination of English society through the lens of the landed gentry.

The theme of friendship is also covered in a sustained way because, of course, there are twenty volumes in the so-called Aubrey-Maturin series that covers a span of time sufficient to allow us to see real development in the two main characters. Jack Aubrey is a big, brash, handsome man of the sea who, unburdened by a classical education, loves to laugh at his own jokes. His unquestioning Naval discipline requires him to live in fear of wasting time, and all aspects of his life are lived 'without the loss of a single minute'. Stephen Maturin is a highly-strung, etiolated medical man, a polymath, an obsessive natural philosopher and a spy. Although Maturin and Aubrey were 'almost as unlike as men could be, unlike in nationality, religion, education, size, shape, profession, habit of mind, they were united in a deep love of music, and many and many an evening had they played together, violin answering cello or both singing together far into the night.'

I decided there and then, on a beach in Zanzibar cut adrift in the Indian Ocean, that I was going to read the lot. I'd read a twenty-book series of novels before – Emile Zola's *Rougon-Macquart* cycle – and I was determined to do it again. Of course, I'd started reading the Aubrey-Maturin series out of sequence, but by the time the monsoons rolled in, I'd read four or five of them on my white beach in Zanzibar and had started to get the hang of them. After several long weeks I was beginning to understand just why O'Brian had such a fearsome reputation. It seemed that his literary achievement could only be appreciated after reaching an understanding about the physical scale of the work. Twenty novels: big novels too, apart from the last few. Let's say they average four hundred pages, with four hundred words per page. That's eight thousand pages, containing in the region of three million words. A tall order indeed, and yet I can honestly say that I never once got even remotely bored, but this might be because I decided to ration them out over four years.

Other reading and writing commitments meant that I could only devote time to O'Brian while on assignment, when there was plenty of dead time in aeroplanes, airports and hotels. I read a couple of them in the mountains of Spain, a couple in a converted incense merchant's house in Morocco. I read *The Fortune of War* in Quebec, *The Far Side of the World* while sailing around the Galapagos, *The Surgeon's Mate* in the Maldives, *The Wine-Dark Sea* in Armenia and *Mauritius Command* on a trip to the Mascarenes. My two favourites – *The Nutmeg of Consolation* and *Clarissa Oakes* – were devoured in Indonesia, while *The Commodore* and *The Letter of the Marque* were dispatched in Lithuania and Iceland respectively. As I reached the end of the sequence I rationed them to strictly one per trip and, when I realised I'd be returning to Zanzibar in the summer of 2004, I decided to orchestrate affairs so that the last volume – *Blue at the Mizzen* – could be read on the same beach as where I'd started, sitting by an old wooden boat beneath a palm tree. I'd travelled the world both on my own and with Patrick O'Brian.

But it seemed that my journey held one last surprise. On my return to the UK in October 2004 I found a brown parcel from HarperCollins on my welcome mat containing O'Brian's *The Final, Unfinished Voyage of Jack Aubrey*. The publisher announced in an accompanying press release that it was poised to 'delight fans by publishing his uncompleted 21st book' before breathlessly suggesting: 'It would be of enormous interest to O'Brien's followers, and indeed all those with an interest in literature, if you would strongly consider commemorating the fascinating and remarkable life of this uniquely talented author.' The release goes on to sigh that the novel sequence comes to an end with Jack sailing through fair, sweet seas and Stephen still dissecting and celebrating a new romance. 'Of course, we'd rather have had the whole story…'

To me it's one of the great mysteries of the trade that O'Brian's novel sequence should be so expensive to collect, with first editions of the early works such as *Post Captain* and *HMS Surprise* commanding colossal sums. It may sound ridiculous, but you could get a whole set of Hornblower firsts for less than, say, a signed first of *Desolation Island*. Obviously, the Aubrey-Maturin series has some terrific attractions for the collector. First, it is a big set with enough widespread material at a reasonable price to get you started. But there are one or two black tulips in there that make the complete set something really worth having. Then there is the issue of the quality of the overall work. The Aubrey-Maturin series is without doubt the finest historical novel sequence I've ever read, and I'll stick my neck out and say that as a novelist O'Brian ranks alongside some of the biggest names you can throw at him from the 20th century. Is he as good as Anthony Powell? Of course he is. D.H.Lawrence? Knocks him into a cocked hat. Graham Greene? Ah well ... Some things are sacred.

But collectors aren't primarily worried about literary value, and will be much more concerned that O'Brian is dead, and has been for a decade. He didn't have a reputation for being a prolific signer, and now the supply is finite and the demand is increasing prices seem, to me at least, to be spiralling out of control. I refuse to collect them, although I did invest in a slip-cased limited and signed edition of his two adolescent novels, *Caesar* and *Hussein*. No, I prefer my well-travelled paperbacks, yellowed and stained by the sea; with cracked spines, turned-down corners, margins filled with notes; with boarding passes as bookmarks ... a real souvenir of a remarkable journey. In the margins I've written notes, sometimes to remind me of a technical point of sea-faring jargon or of the common name of a specimen under dissection by Stephen. But at other times it's no more than a grunt of approval, reserved for when O'Brian gets the poised detachment of maturing friendship so brilliantly spot on. If you held a gun to my head, probably I'd confess to preferring Jack to Stephen, whose wide-eyed lust for life is so irrepressible, whose humour is so easy. I'd always liked his much-repeated gag about the 'lesser of two weevils', but there is a moment in one of the middle novels – I forget which – where after much claret with his officers the captain guilelessly explains why he feels so sorry for Americans. 'They're republicans *and* democrats,' he explains with good-natured despair. Perhaps it's time to pay a visit to the cellar and dig out my old copies of this greatest of seafaring *romans-fleuve*, without, as Jack Aubrey would have said, 'the loss of a minute'.

CHAPTER 33

A place I've never been

I WAS IN SUCH a rush to get to the airport that I forgot to pack anything to read. That's not quite true. I had tucked away the instruction manual of my new digital camera as well as a stack of my daughter's bedtime story books, including a stupendous new edition of *Goldilocks and the Three Bears* by Lauren Child. But, I had completely neglected to pack what we used to call in school a 'reading book'.

As the plane drifted over the Mediterranean towards Mount Sinai, where I'd been sent to photograph St Catherine's monastery, I decided that this might be no bad thing. I really needed to catch up on my homework, to find out what buttons did what on my recently acquired Canon 5D MkII. As I flicked through the booklet I marvelled at why precision instrument manufacturers supply such awful documentation with their ground-breaking technology. These terrible manuals are always 'authored by technical writers' rather than written by technical authors. And while I'm not entirely sure what a technical author is, a friend of mine, who is technically an author, tells me that they're translated by monkeys.

After a few minutes of 'bite the wax tadpole' type hilarity, it occurred to me that the book in my hands wasn't worth the slaughter of innocent trees. And while it's probably good for the soul of all photographers to check up on how their new machine copes with the setting of exposure compensation increment levels, I almost certainly wasn't going to find any answer that I could understand here. I returned the manual to my camera bag and for the remainder of the flight tried to read *The Day of the Triffids* over the shoulder of a young woman who, unhappy with the arrangement, tried her hardest to turn away from me in such a way that wouldn't make her look rude. Which was odd, because I was the one being rude.

Eventually we landed in Sharm El Sheikh, the once tiny fishing village in the fork of the 'Y' at the north end of the Red Sea, where today multitudes of overweight Russians and leathery Germans gather to take their winter holidays. I checked into my hotel and began the instinctive ritual of scanning around for a bookshop. But there wasn't one, unless you count a small book exchange where the cracked, dog-eared paperbacks of Alistair MacLean, Dennis Wheatley and Jean Plaidy had evidently all gone to die. There was a copy of *Silas Marner*, but since completing *Middlemarch* at the age of nineteen I'd managed to keep my life mercifully free from George Eliot, and I didn't want to destroy a fine run of form simply because I was desperate for something to read. I smiled as I remembered W.H. Auden's limerick that went, if I can remember it properly, something like this:

T.S. Eliot is quite at a loss
When clubwomen bustle across
At literary teas
Crying: 'What, if you please,
Did you mean by *The Mill on the Floss?*'

My infant's bedtime came and went, and as much as I
have come to love Katherine Holabird and Helen Craig's
'Angelina Ballerina' books – an exquisitely illustrated series
of cautionary tales for the very young, whose protagonist
is a ballet-dancing mouse – they really weren't going to
make the long Egyptian winter night pass quickly, no
matter how balmy and star strewn. I glanced forlornly at the
boxed set of the chronicles of Narnia that I'd brought along
in the hope that I could interest my five-year-old in what
had been my favourite childhood books. Once the infant
had dropped off to sleep, I raided the mini-bar, knocked up
a stiff bourbon and coke and wandered into the fantastic,
glorious, wonderful world of Narnia for the first time in
decades.

I know these days in our boring secular politically
correct society it's become fashionable to dislike C.S. Lewis
and everything he stands for. One of our most important
children's storytellers, Philip Pullman, has said that he finds
the Narnia books 'a peevish blend of racist, misogynistic and
reactionary prejudice' without 'a trace' of Christian charity.
Of course, the author of the *His Dark Materials* trilogy has
a point: the dullest of moderately competent English literature undergraduates would have no problem proving it
either. I remember with some embarrassment once writing
that in Lewis's invented world of Narnia it often seems as

though it's better to be a boy than a girl. You could go one further and say that he thought it better to be a Christian than a Muslim, a talking animal than a dumb beast, better to be dead than alive.

There are bags of examples, and here are a few drawn from memory. In *The Lion, the Witch and the Wardrobe*, when the Pevensie children fulfil the ancient prophecy and are crowned at Cair Paravel, it's Peter who is made High King. In *The Magician's Nephew* it's Digory who has to rescue Polly from the Wood between the Worlds. The Christ-like Aslan says that the battlefield is 'no place for a woman'. In *The Horse and His Boy* the Calormenes – who with their crimson-dyed beards, turbans and pointy slippers are clearly meant to represent the 'infidel' – are presented as harsh and cruel, living by a law more concerned with justice than forgiveness. In *The Last Battle* the Calormene god Tash has a 'deathly smell', while 'the grass seemed to whither beneath it'. The rather buck-ho Jill Pole calls Tash 'that thing'. In *The Voyage of the Dawn Trader*, Reepicheep, king of the talking mice (who are the size of small dogs), continually proclaims his disdain for his dumb cousins, while in *The Horse and His Boy* we are lectured on what an honour it is for Shasta and Aravis to ride talking horses, because in Narnia only dumb animals can be beasts of burden. Finally – and this is the bit that really annoys Pullman – there is the issue of the worldly Susan being denied salvation, while her brothers, sister and cousins all make their triumphant way to paradise – in this case literally a walled garden – where they settle joyfully into life eternal 'in which every chapter is better than the one before'.

But none of this qualifies as remarkable insight. I'm far more interested in why the books maintain their appeal despite their alleged flaws and faults. The real reason why critics today dislike the Narnia books is that they can't quite work out what to do with the overtly Christian message they convey. They become hyperventilated over the supposedly allegorical nature of the Narnian Heptateuch. They become nervous about the resurrection on the Stone Table and the salvation of the Stable. But the truth is that the books aren't allegorical at all, in the accepted categories of literal, typological, moral or anagogical. We know this because Lewis was a leading expert on allegory – his *The Allegory of Love* was required reading while I was studying medieval English at Oxford – and he said that they weren't, and that's good enough for me. As Lewis famously wrote in a letter to a Mrs Hook in December 1958:

> If Aslan represented the immaterial Deity in the same way in which Giant Despair represents despair, he would be an allegorical figure. In reality however he is an invention giving an imaginary answer to the question, 'What might Christ become like, if there really were a world like Narnia and He chose to be incarnate and die and rise again in that world as He actually has done in ours?' This is not allegory at all.

The point is a fine one, and it may be that Lewis, who wrote some of the finest Christian apologia of the 20th century, has a charitably high opinion of the ability of the layman to pick over the bones of complex theosophical issues such as these. But this doesn't help us to understand why *The Lion, the Witch and the Wardrobe* and its six sequels (okay, one is a prequel) should have maintained their popularity. Although I'm not a psychologist, I think part of the answer may lie in there being two very different men in C.S. Lewis competing to write these books. First there was the other-worldly Oxford academic, writer of complex tracts on abstract and arcane matters such as whether the Renaissance actually happened, the nature of miracles, Christian ethics, morality and grief. Then there was the bufferish old don who liked a pint of beer, smoked a pipe and loved laughter; wrote lousy science fiction and, although he knew next to nothing of children, concocted fantasies that he assumed might appeal to them.

And appeal to us he did. His epic stories of heroic battles where noble warriors wore armour and chainmail, of a land where it was 'always winter, but never Christmas', where deep magic from the dawn of time was trumped by even deeper magic from before the dawn of time, have powerful roots in the ancient art of telling a decent story properly (something the makers of the lamentable movie version of *Prince Caspian* might have done well to have taken note of). As a child I was drawn to the nobility of the values that set aside good from evil, instinctively understanding why the fauns and the dryads and the marsh-wiggles were in the right, while the hags and the werewolves and the wooses (yes, there really were wooses in Narnia) were not only wrong, but needed to be given a good hiding, six-of-the-best, trousers down. And if that all sounds a little like the expulsion from Eden then who cares, because the stories fairly rattled along with pace, action and excitement. For all the shouting critics ranting that youngsters were being indoctrinated with bible stories, I've not read one that's ever noticed, complained or cared about Lewis paying as much attention, if not more, to hammering home the five knightly virtues of generosity, courtesy, chastity, chivalry and piety that we find in *Sir Gawain and the Green Knight.*

But the biggest attraction of all was simply that you could never go to Narnia. Even today, as I travel the world photographing some of the rarest wildlife, poetically beautiful landscapes and most far-flung people, I get really frustrated that I simply can't just board a plane to this mythical medieval land. The harsh, romantic reality is that – as with Tolkien's Middle Earth and Ursula Le Guin's Earthsea – Narnia is an invented topography that will remain forever elusive, no matter how many wardrobes you open. And this is why for me, despite what Philip Pullman says, these are wonderful books of the imagination. And as for those who don't agree? Well, they're simply trendy killjoys and I despair of them.

With the required photographs of St Catherine's monastery in the bag, I watched the sandstone desert outcrops slide past the bus window as we meandered in the setting sun to Sharm El Sheikh. Having dispatched the last of my *Telegraph* crosswords with an almost contemptuous flick of the quill, I found myself curiously absorbed in my new copy of *The Day of the Triffids* that I'd picked up off an aeroplane seat a few days before. As I read the fantastically named John Wyndham Parkes Lucas Benyon Harris's apocalyptic tale of genetic modification, social disintegration and brimstone Gehenna, I found it hard to believe that this ultra-modern parabolic novel was published in 1951, just a year after *The Lion, the Witch and the Wardrobe.* And, despite the obvious and polar differences, they have similarities that go beyond the walking plants that seemed to be so popular in 1950s fiction. I wondered if the idea of a man removing the bandages from his eyes to discover that flesh-eating flora had gained an evolutionary advantage in a post-Armageddon society was so very different from being transported to a different world altogether, where the fabric of morality is put to the test by the uprising of evil. What's more, I think Lewis's classic is just as plausible as Wyndham's.

Writing from their post-Second-World-War perspective, where Wyndham saw chaos and violence, Lewis saw at least the opportunity for conciliation and redemption. And, while both writers were successful, it's my view that the opti-mistic and life-affirming Narnia books will still be read in a hundred years' time, while *The Day of the Triffids*, along with *The Kraken Wakes*, *The Chrysalids* and the *Midwich Cuckoos* will be largely forgotten. This is not because these hugely influential works had nothing to say, but because – as with Lewis's own science fiction – the doomsday scenarios they comment upon will have either failed to materialise or will somehow have been avoided. On the other hand, the classic and enduring moral dilemmas that form the core of the Narnia books will be confronting children of every age in the future, whatever the future.

214

CHAPTER 34

A Woolf in
the jungles of Ceylon

THERE'S NOTHING like a spot of overseas travel for dishing up bizarre coincidences. I know we shouldn't make too much of coincidences because, as with solar eclipses, most of the time they don't happen at all and, what's more, we don't notice them not happening. As a friend of mine wrote in a recent novel: 'If time is the means by which the universe prevents everything from happening at once, coincidence is the excuse it uses when things occasionally do.' The sensible response to which is to say, 'I couldn't agree more,' but it was nonetheless a coincidence as splendid as the alignment of celestial orbs that I should be reading Leonard Woolf's *The Village in the Jungle* when the plane I was on succumbed to a 'technical' and was diverted to Sri Lanka, where it is set.

This was back in 2004. I'd been asked to write a critical introduction – in the sense that I analyse the text rather than produce something indispensable – for a new edition of the novel and decided to take my research with me on assignment to the Maldives where, for the record, I was photographing juvenile black-tip reef sharks for a wildlife magazine. As I read about the jungles of old Ceylon, I could see what's left of them in 21st-century Sri Lanka through the porthole. And, although I was worried that I might never make it to the necklace of islands that Marco Polo called the 'flower of the Indes', I was held spellbound by the brilliance of Woolf's prose.

Oddly enough, as the plane landed on the pear-shaped island, it was exactly – almost to the day – a century after the young Leonard Woolf sailed from his native Britain to Ceylon. Having just come down from Cambridge, the gifted barrister's son was heading eastward to serve a term as a colonial administrator in the Civil Service. It was a journey that was to take Woolf away from his Jewish London roots for seven years, but more significantly it was to transform him from an ensconced imperialist to a radical anti-imperialist. The views he developed while serving in Ceylon were to be influential to the thinking of the Fabian Society and the Labour Party in the years leading up to the Second World War.

In his new role in the Civil Service, Woolf came to know much about the fabric of Ceylon, and it's this deep knowledge that informs every page of *The Village in the Jungle*, his first and best novel. Although he drank gin and tonic in the elevated and strictly hierarchical society of the British expats, he also took the time to get to know the ways of the Sinhalese, how they thought and worked, as well as the exotic charms of the local burgher women. While he reluctantly played tennis with his fellow instruments of Empire, he also embraced the extraordinary workload inflicted upon him by a regime built on the bureaucratic process.

Work was the real issue and defining characteristic of Woolf's Ceylon years – something that was to serve him well in later life. He was a slave to his own punishing work ethic: his ability to 'stick at it' was an important factor in his meteoric rise to influence in Ceylon. He did the work of his superiors in Jaffna; organised social events in Kandy with great efficiency for Sir Hugh Clifford – the acting Governor of Ceylon (and a notorious womaniser) – and was rewarded with the Assistant Government Agent job in Hambantota, the youngest civil servant ever to be appointed to the post. Woolf's efficiency and industry in the dry southeast Hambantota area resulted in the district being the best-run region in Ceylon. He doubled salt production as he had doubled the pearl-fishing profits during an earlier posting in Jaffna.

His time in Ceylon was so significant to Woolf that he devoted the entire second volume of his five-book auto-biography to it. Called *Growing*, it's one of those books you want to read again and again. Of course I'm fascinated by the minutiae of his life and his opinions on the creaking structure of Empire, but what I like best is his effortlessness with the English language. The act of writing seems to have come to him as easily as blowing a penny whistle, and when-ever I feel clogged up by overwritten text (normally my own) I instinctively turn to Leonard Woolf to remind me that the best way to say something is simply. It's always a bookish pleasure to return to his autobiography because my copies are all firsts that I bought a few years back for around £200. I remember at the time thinking that this was probably a little too much, but they were in such good condition and I've never regretted the purchase.

Although serious, intelligent and often highbrow, Woolf is also often very funny. At the beginning of *Growing* he describes his relationship with fashion as well as his dog. He wears a ludicrous green collar (Woolf, not the dog) calculated to draw accusations of foppishness that he then passes off as unaffected eccentricity. The dog is a stage prop he uses to bolster his masculinity. The dog fights, escapes, runs fast and is exciting. The somewhat avian Woolf sincerely believes that he'll absorb these attributes simply through the passive act of owning the canine. He knows he's being funny, revels in provoking laughter, and you should read it.

While Woolf was gaining his administrative experience, he was also soaking up the raw material for his novel. He was a meticulous diarist with a journalist's eye for detail, and many of the descriptive passages in *The Village in the Jungle* are taken straight from his diaries. He was also sympathetic to the plight of the locals and had a flair for diplomacy that meant he was able to balance the demands of Empire with treating the local people fairly.

This all came together in 1913 when Woolf, now back in the UK, published *The Village in the Jungle*. As novels go it's a remarkably straightforward murder story. No subplot and very little literary artifice to speak of – just that lovely controlled, slightly rhythmic and occasionally musical voice of his. The murder triggers an examination of colonial oppression and its effect on a remote settlement in a pocket of dense forest. Woolf called his village Beddagama, which is Sinhala, where 'baddha' means 'village' and 'gama' is 'jungle'. Woolf claimed it had no prototype, but one notable Woolf expert – Christopher Ondaatje – thinks it does.

During his many excursions on administrative business Woolf noticed how villages rise and fall with the moods of the jungle. When the monsoon arrives on time a village will prosper: there is rice to be grown, and the villagers have enough energy to keep their compounds clear, and work their small stockaded fields called *chenas*. But when it is in decline, the jungle drains the will of the people before swallowing the village whole, as happens with Beddagama. The jungle is a fearful place and Woolf's opening description is amazing:

> For the rule of the jungle is first fear, and then hunger and thirst. There is fear everywhere … And behind the fear is always the hunger and the thirst, and behind the hunger and the thirst fear again.

When I first read this I immediately thought of that bit in *The Second Jungle Book* where Kipling writes,

> Now this is the Law of the Jungle – as old and as true as
> the sky;
> And the Wolf that shall keep it may prosper,
> But the Wolf that shall break it must die.

But it's not just the Kipling echo that gives this passage such resonance. There's also Woolf's rhythmic repetition and rhyme that reminds us that the poems of T.S. Eliot are only a few years down the track. The influence of Eliot on

Woolf (and vice versa) shouldn't be underestimated. As the head of the Hogarth Press, Woolf took 'great pleasure' in publishing Eliot's poems, including, in 1923, one of the defining poems of the post-war world, 'The Waste Land'.

The best book about Woolf's years on the colonial outpost is Christopher Ondaatje's biography *Woolf in Ceylon: An Imperial Journey in the Shadow of Leonard Woolf 1904-1911* and I said as much when I was asked to write on it in the *Literary Review* in 2005. In it Ondaatje contends that the novel's importance lies primarily in its being one of the few pre-First-World-War fictional works to deal with a colonial situation from the perspective of the *colonised* rather than the *coloniser* – a blatant clue as to Woolf's developing revulsion at what he saw as the injustice of imperialism. Ondaatje performs some literary forensics as he sets out to find the original village of the title and, working on the basis that Woolf's fiction is nearly always rooted in fact, he assumes that the double murder central to the novel's plot must have happened in a real place. True to his explorer's instincts, Ondaatje not only finds the actual site of Beddagama, but also links the murders and Woolf to it.

It may be an indication of how rich Woolf's life was, but in her 2006 biography *Leonard Woolf: A Life,* Victoria Glendinning virtually passes over the author's first novel entirely, devoting to it a mere five pages out of a total of well over 500. What little she does have to say, however, raises two interesting points: first, that there had been scarcely any critical attention focused on *The Village in the Jungle* until Woolf's death in 1969. This can be dealt with by saying that it's no great revelation that Woolf's been creatively overshadowed by his wife Virginia, who had ensured her cult status by committing suicide in 1941. As a result, her first novel *The Voyage Out* is often seen as more important than her husband's.

Glendinning's second point is that what little critical attention there had been was more concerned with Woolf's political stance than the literary success or otherwise of his book. Glendinning wonders if *The Village in the Jungle* is 'an anti-imperialist text, or a paternalistic and imperialist text', which in turn makes me wonder if there might be a few pages missing from her copy. When the jungle is used as a metaphor for the encroachment of Empire, it devours all in its way. 'All jungles are evil, but no jungle is more evil than that which lay about the village of Beddagama.' When Empire must pass judgment on the central character Silindu, in what is effectively the climax of the story, Empire loses its nerve. 'All he wanted was to be left alone, poor devil,' says the court magistrate when pondering the possibility of having to hang Silindu for the murders. The issue of the white man vacillating, unable to take the upper hand, concerned one critic of the time.

Lytton Strachey, who was a friend of Woolf and a contemporary at Cambridge, famously disliked *The Village in the Jungle* because of its over-concern with the fortunes of 'the blacks' and urged Woolf to include in his next novel 'Whites! Whites! Whites!' Whatever Strachey's views of *The Village in the Jungle*, Woolf could see the cracks that heralded the disintegration of Empire.

The unrelenting claustrophobia of the jungle and the sense of doom and inevitability contained in every descriptive passage of his novel have led some commentators to compare Woolf with Thomas Hardy. And while it is true that Hardy's bleaker works – such as *Tess of the D'Urbervilles* and *Jude the Obscure* – share with Woolf the belief in the pointlessness of struggling against a fate indifferent to human suffering, this is where the resemblance stops. Woolf is far more concerned with colonial occupation than inevitability, and concerned with the jungle as a symbol for the enclosing and engulfing colonising forces of the British Empire. This is in fact much closer to Joseph Conrad's treatment of the jungle in *The Heart of Darkness*. Conrad's story is set in the Belgian Congo (today's Democratic Republic of the Congo) and he uses his jungle in Africa to convey the horrors of colonial oppression (as an aside, T.S. Eliot originally chose Conrad's famous 'The horror! the horror!' as the epigraph to 'The Waste Land' before rejecting it in favour of a quotation from Petronius's *Satyricon*).

As his ship docked in Colombo, Woolf could hardly have known that the years of colonial administration ahead of him were to produce one of the finest pieces of literature written in English about Ceylon (W.T. Keble's *Ceylon Beaten Track*, published in 1940, is another much-loved account of old Ceylon). It's been translated into Sinhalese and has never been out of print in Sri Lanka, where it's regarded as a national treasure. That *The Village in the Jungle* hasn't yet been received into the canon of the greats of English literature is something of a mystery, but with a current revival of interest in Woolf that includes two recent biographies and several new editions of his fiction, admission can surely be only a matter of time.

As *The Village in the Jungle* approaches its centenary there is one final irony, and that is that this atmospheric book has outlived the jungle it portrays. As you fly over Sri Lanka today, the dense forest that once made this island a tangled, impenetrable mass of choking vegetation has been all but cleared away. Once we were powerless to resist the advances of nature, but now technology has allowed us to gain a different kind of imperialist upper hand, and so the jungle has been cut down in order to make way for agriculture and 'development'. The colonial administrator Woolf would have admired the efficiency and rapidity with which this has been achieved, but the deeply sensitive and poetic man who could make words sound like music would have hated the very thought of it.

CHAPTER 35

Beating about the bush

I T ALL STARTED in a cobbled town square in Armenia's
capital Yerevan, where I once had a drink with a rather
mustachioed newspaper editor. Armenian brandy is
quite good and very cheap, so before long Kieran and I gave
up all attempts at civilised conversation and started playing
the sort of parlour games you only play once you've reached
a certain condition.

Being seasoned travel writers, we managed to get the fifty
states of America between us in, if not record time, then
something bordering on it. But then Kieran threw in a real
curve ball. 'Okay,' he drawled eyeing the remains of the
bottle with deep suspicion, 'how many countries in Africa
can you name?' I scratched my head and started. After about
five – and this included Egypt, Kenya and South Africa – I
dried up, hopelessly lost. 'I can name them all,' he said.

And he did. Well, I can't be absolutely certain about this,
but his list issued forth fluently and effortlessly. By the time
he'd folded his arms behind his head, rocked back on the
hind legs of his chair and polished off his brandy, his tally

was more than fifty, including several – such as Burundi, Mauritania and Western Sahara – that at the time I'd never heard of. 'How do you know all these?' I asked, impressed. 'Oh, I used to live there,' he said.

When pushed, he told me that he'd once owned a farm in Kenya. It was called 'Ayadah'. I asked him if this was Swahili for anything in particular and he looked at me with mildly condescending half-closed eyes as if to wonder whether I knew anything about anything. 'They're the first words of the best book about Kenya, dear boy,' he said.

'I had a farm in Africa at the foot of the Ngong Hills,' he intoned in an accent I later came to realise was an attempt at impersonating Meryl Streep. As we all now know, thanks to the 1985 Oscar-winning movie, this is Karen Blixen's opening line from her memoir *Out of Africa*. And while earning his living on a farm in an adjacent part of Kenya, Kieran had made a point of travelling around as much of the Dark Continent as he could. Perhaps he liked having a passport full of stamps – the type you no longer get these days. I know I do. Perhaps he just had Africa in his blood.

Funnily enough I've been there, I told him, referring to what's now the Karen Blixen Museum, an Independence gift from the Danish Government to Kenya. I'd been on assignment to Kenya in the late 1990s and found myself with time on my hands in Nairobi before heading south to the Masai Mara for a swanky interiors magazine whose name I've forgotten. My guide had offered me the choice of the elephant orphanage, giraffe centre or crocodile farm. Those or Karen Blixen's house – but you don't want to go there, said my guide, who from the minute we got there slept in his car. Maybe he was right, because Blixen's house isn't very interesting or even particularly authentic. The mahogany panels evoke an air of yesteryear to be sure, and there are Denys Finch-Hatton's books decaying in the humid African air. There's even a pair of Blixen's boots by her bed ... except they're the boots Meryl wore in the movie and the bed is a stage property donated by Universal Studios. All the real stuff is elsewhere, either in Blixen's native Denmark or in private collections.

These are the reflections I was enjoying while airborne on my way to Nairobi a few weeks ago on assignment for the *Daily Telegraph*. This time it was going to be different, as I'd made the decision to avoid the much-visited south in favour of exploring the isolated northern regions. I also had a reading list provided by my thoughtful travel agents, and as I flicked through I made a mental note of those I'd already read. My heart sank when I discovered that first up was Wilfred Thesiger's *My Kenya Days*. Apart from being quite dull, the book wasn't even written by the explorer himself, but dictated later in life to his amanuensis Alexander Maitland. The claim has always been that Thesiger dictated the book on account of his failing eyesight, but the truth is that Thesiger was never much of a writer, his earlier books having been edited to the point of being rewritten by the likes of Valentine ffrench-Blake and Gavin Young. This isn't to say that I don't like his earlier books – *Arabian Sands* and *The Marsh Arabs* are quite good – it's just that I couldn't find anything positive to say about *My Kenya Days* when I reviewed it. In fact I accused it of being little more than 'a beefed-up diary', duly gave it the critical raspberry, and with the passing of time I see no need to change my opinion.

Apparently, while dictating his book on location, Thesiger would march up and down declaiming in his sonorous baritone, occasionally pausing to ask Maitland if he was bored. In a recent interview Maitland said: 'I never was. It was amazing watching it happen, it was like sitting with George Eliot.' It would be unkind to make the obvious joke here, and possibly unwise too, because every time I've ever dared to suggest – and I've done so in the *Literary Review* and the *Times Higher Education Supplement* – that Thesiger's books might be anything less than masterpieces, I've drawn fire from the exploration establishment.

More promising was the inclusion on the list of Joy Adamson's *Born Free*. The book, the movie and even Matt Monro's rendition of John Barry's theme song all evoke in me a sentimental picture of Kenya, one of bush omelets under acacia trees, G&Ts in the sunset with a copy of John le Carré's *The Constant Gardener* to hand. Based on her notes and husband George's diaries, *Born Free* was published in 1960 and went to number one on the *New York Times* bestseller list. Beautifully illustrated with dozens of photographs of the lion cub Elsa, this spellbinding tale is probably, for most of us, our first introduction to wildlife conservation. Well received by the literary critics but, much more importantly, loved by children the world over, this was the book that launched the Born Free Foundation, a wildlife charity that helps to prevent animal suffering and protects threatened species. A highly amusing (for several reasons)

Wikipedia entry explains that 'while Joy Adamson generously shared book proceeds with various conservation projects, she showed no such generousity [sic] with [sic] her husband George from whom she had separated.'

Perhaps the most prolific writer on Kenya was the little-known Elspeth Huxley, a relation by marriage of the more famous Aldous, whose *Brave New World* is an enduring classic. Elspeth grew up as a 'Kenya cowgirl' on a coffee farm, not unlike Karen Blixen's, managed by her father, an experience she describes in her autobiographical fiction *The Flame Trees of Thika* and *The Mottled Lizard*. While for many Kenyans today these are old-fashioned lyrical cele-brations of colonial rule, they're still enjoyed for their rich humour, affectionate personal portraits and Huxley's gentle evocation of life as a white settler. Immensely popular at the time, *The Flame Trees of Thika* was made into a television series.

If my list had started with a whimper, then it ended with a bang of sorts, in the form of a couple of gun-toting Hemingway standards, *Snows of Kilimanjaro* and *Green Hills of Africa*. The former is most remarkable in that it was a set text on my school syllabus, while the latter is a dreary journal of a month-long safari where Hemingway took delight in blowing the heads off unsuspecting kudu. One critic at the time wrote that it was 'the best-written story of big-game hunting anywhere I have read. And more than that. It's a book about people in unacknowledged conflict and about the pleasures of travel and the pleasures of drink-ing and war and peace and writing.' Hemingway famously said that the critics had 'killed' his book and immediately slumped into a depression, and in what some might be prepared to see as poetic justice declared himself 'ready to blow my lousy head off'. In Jack Kerouac's *On the Road* Roland Major says, 'Have you ever read *Green Hills of Africa*? It's Hemingway's best.' He's wrong.

For my money the only serious contender to rank alongside *Out of Africa* is J.H. Patterson's *The Man-Eaters of Tsavo*, which deals with his experiences a century ago while overseeing the construction of a railway bridge on the Tsavo River in what's now Kenya. Shortly after the arrival of Colonel John Henry Patterson DSO there was a spate of lion attacks, with railway workers dragged from tents at night and eaten by the predators. Despite the building of *bomas* around the camps, the lighting of bonfires and strict curfews, the raids escalated and work on the bridge came to a halt as the suspicious local work-force refused point blank to carry on. Faced with the challenge of maintaining his authority, Patterson – an experienced tiger hunter who'd cut his teeth in India – was left with no option but to track down the big cats, and in December 1898 he killed them both. The local people immediately declared Patterson a hero, returned to work with renewed vigour, and the Tsavo railway bridge was completed in February 1899. I've always liked *The Man-Eaters of Tsavo* and it's almost as good as anything by the great man-eater specialist Jim Corbett, and that's saying something.

After what seemed like a sleepless lifetime on the long, bumpy 'bed and breakfast' flight to Nairobi, we landed in an equatorial storm. I paid my twenty-five bucks for a visa at Jomo Kenyatta airport and transferred to Wilson, where I caught a 16-seater light aircraft north. Eventually, we landed on a red earthen airstrip where I was met by Andrew Francombe, who flew me an hour westwards in his tiny Cessna to his family ranch at Ol Malo. As we passed low over a brown, muddy river I took some aerial shots of herds of elephant and camel trains. When we reached our final destination we sat by his swimming pool high on top of a volcanic kopje, drinking ice-cold Kilimanjaro beer. Andrew wanted to know why I'd come so far off the beaten track, and so I told him that I'd lost interest in the tourist traps down south and wanted this time to get to grips with the wild country up north of the Equator.

But my burning question for Andrew was whether we'd get to see any big cats. Oh sure, came the reply, there are leopard here at the moment. And then I asked him if he'd ever seen a black leopard. Yes, he said, there's one around somewhere. Taken aback by his nonchalance, I told him of an article I'd once published in *Geographical* magazine by the explorer Christopher Ondaatje – 'The Riddle of Lewa Downs' – in which the author had travelled extensively throughout northern Kenya in pursuit of the elusive melanistic panther.

Although Ol Malo is on the Laikipia Plain, we were in roughly the same neck of the woods as where Ondaatje had tracked the animal – one of the rarest on the planet – and shot some shaky, but conclusive video footage. Andrew looked at me in some amazement. 'Yes,' he said. 'I know that story, and I know that animal.' I asked how he knew it was the same one and he told me there had only been two of these handsome black leopards in the region in his lifetime, and one of them had died many years ago. 'The one in Laikipia,' he said, 'came from Lewa Downs. There have been sightings, but they're few and far between.' At this point Andrew's father explained: 'It's a sign of rain, you know. No doubt about it. That cat's bound to bring rain with it.' I told my hosts that, as far as I could remember, in 'The Riddle of Lewa Downs' the black leopard was an ill omen, a harbinger of drought. At this they laughed. 'Everything to these old guys,' said Andrew, 'is a sign of rain or drought. The way the elephant stands. The time the tawny eagle chooses to build its nest. The baboon spider hiding in the earth. The only thing we wait for is the rains and the only thing we fear is drought.'

Something about this incident impressed me on a level I find hard to explain. Maybe it was that I could fly halfway around the world to the greatest wide open space there is, only to find that the big cat I'd read about in the Royal Geographical Society in Kensington could be the very one we were talking about as the sun set behind the flat top acacias. Maybe it was that without knowing it I'd once again been lured into a far-flung adventure by a few words on the page of a book. We didn't get to see the black leopard of course, but that hardly mattered. After a few days I said goodbye to my hosts and flew back to Nairobi.

Finding myself once again with time to kill I get a cab and go back to Karen Blixen's house, where nothing's changed. But that's the nature of museums I tell myself as I hunt in the souvenir shop for something to read on the long flight home. A lucky find, I settle on a dusty old copy of Jim Corbett's *Man-Eaters of Kumaon* and decide that my next peregrination should be in India. A few hours out of Nairobi we make an unscheduled stop at Khartoum in Sudan where the wife of a Kenyan government official is removed from the plane in order to give birth. After all these adventures, I don't find this remotely odd. Perhaps it's just me.

The Devil's in the detail

I've always been a huge fan of Ian Fleming and so to bump into his nephew Fergus – an accomplished author on Polar affairs – was an unexpected and very bookish treat. But try as I might, I simply couldn't get the material to work as a col-umn for Bookdealer *and it ended up as one of those occasional features that gets published simply because it's interesting. Well I think so, which is why I've included it in* Travels in the World of Books, *despite it not quite fulfilling all the qualification requirements.*

'I DO IT ALL on the typewriter, using six fingers,' says Ian Fleming in his new book *Talk of the Devil*, explaining how he writes his novels. The thriller writer most famous for creating James Bond has been dead for forty-five years, but there's still enough 'little seen material, some of it unpublished' knocking around to warrant this new collection. It's been compiled from rarities in the Fleming archive and, at more than 400 pages, is the longest work ever to bear the author's name. Its editors are Fleming's nephew Fergus Fleming and niece Kate Grimond, both of whom are directors of the Fleming literary estate and are writers in their own right. The cousins also jointly manage Queen Anne Press, which is responsible for the Ian Fleming Centenary Edition: an 18-volume collected works published to commemorate what would be the author's 100th birthday. Incredibly, it is the first complete, uniform edition of Fleming's work ever to go on sale, and it's the only way you'll get hold of a copy of *Talk of the Devil*, for the time being at least. If you want to buy a set of the strictly limited finely bound edition you'll need to disburse in the order of £14,000. A less ostentatious, but nonetheless beautiful cloth-bound version limited to 250 sets comes in at, all things considered, a very reasonable £2,000.

It's all come full circle because Fleming was once managing director of Queen Anne Press, having received it as a wedding gift from the then proprietor of the *Sunday Times*, Lord Kemsley, who in 1952 gave it to his famous Foreign Editor. The publishing house, which was created to publish the works of notable authors, has since gone through many incarnations, but with its recent acquisition by the Fleming estate it is once again fulfilling its original mission, even if *Talk of the Devil* is posthumous. The books are being sold through selected antiquarian dealers such as Henry Sotheran (where the edition was launched in October 2008) and Adrian Harrington, who can justly claim to be one of the foremost authorities in Flemingabilia. They've already started doing the rounds of the trade fairs, and they're also being sold by word of mouth. In fact, I first became aware of Fergus's hands-on approach to selling the edition when I saw him 'door stepping' in Curzon Street, coming out of Heywood Hill with a set of prospectuses under his arm.

'Kate was the driving force behind the project,' says Fergus. 'I got involved really because she was going to see the printers and asked if I would like to come along.' Now he's involved up to his neck, and looks genuinely surprised when he informs me that 'selling books does take up a surprising amount of time'. Of course, flogging fancy Bond books isn't his main job. When not touting the set door-to-door in Mayfair, Fergus is a writer of critically acclaimed narrative non-fiction, perhaps best known for exploration titles including *Barrow's Boys*, *Ninety Degrees North: the Quest for the North Pole* and *Killing Dragons: the Conquest of the Alps*.

His uncle could write a bit too, and although we know Ian Fleming as the creator of Bond, he was also a serious bibliophile. In the 1930s he amassed a collection of first editions covering landmarks in human achievement or which changed the course of history: Karl Marx's *Manifesto*, Alexander Graham Bell's *Researches into Telephony*, Sigmund Freud's *Die Traumdeutung* (*The Interpretation of Dreams*), Francis Galton's *Finger Prints* and more. His library was considered so important that it was evacuated during the Blitz. In 1963 the British Library held an exhibition called 'Printing and the Mind of Man' to which Fleming was the largest private contributor, loaning some 600 volumes. His books were contained in black boxes stamped in gold with the family crest, as is the Queen Anne Press edition. Fleming's collection is now held by the Lilly Library, University of Indiana, along with the first editions of his own novels.

The Centenary Edition consists of eighteen volumes in all: twelve James Bond novels, two collections of Bond short stories, one children's book, two volumes of journalism and finally *Talk of the Devil*. The edition is available in three formats, each strictly limited: a finely bound set, a vellum set and a cloth set, all bound by Shepherds, Sangorski and Sutcliffe, who have just acquired additional premises in Curzon Street, opposite Heywood Hill. 'Rob Shepherd has been extremely helpful,' says Fergus, 'at every stage of our learning curve … learning precipice, more like.'

The bindings for the first set are in contemporary leather designed by Webb & Webb, with leather inlays and even the occasional piece of treasure set into a dark blue background (apparently Fleming's favourite colour). The vellum set is based on a design the author came up with for a special edition of *On Her Majesty's Secret Service*. The cloth set has polished leather plaques on the spines, tooled with the 'scrambled egg' insignia of a Royal Navy Commander, the rank Fleming held during the war and which he later conferred on Bond. The books have been completely reset by Libanus Press, keeping the original period oddities and expressions, but 'getting rid of the typos'. Everything about the edition has a connection to Fleming. Even the body copy font – Fournier – is connected, Fournier of course being the name of whom Fergus describes as 'Fleming's sister's most influential lover'. This is something all parties are prepared to admit might only be truly appreciated by the more thorough Fleming aficionado.

The finely-bound sets are broken up into two categories: the first is of 26 (lettered A-Z) while another 30 are lettered according to the Russian alphabet, the idea being that some collectors would like the set with their own initial and, as Cyrillic has many letters in common with Roman, this will give collectors a second bite of the cherry. As Fleming explains: 'So if, say, F for Freddie has gone in the first set, then ... well actually you can't do that because there's no F in Russian, but if say B for Boris had gone...' In the Russian category, set 'M' has been removed and likewise '007' from the numbered (001-100) vellum sets. 'These are the two most prestigious associations, so we thought we'd auction them for charity,' says Fergus.

Apart from the Bond books, there are four others. *Thrilling Cities* is a volume of travel writing, in which the publishers have been careful to incorporate the original illustrations of Milton Glaser, the New York designer famous for the I♥NY logo. *Thrilling Cities* is a collection of his travel journalism published in the *Sunday Times* over the years, a genre in which Fleming was overshadowed by his older brother Peter, a noted explorer and author of classics such *News from Tartary* and *Brazilian Adventure*.

Relatively obscure, *The Diamond Smugglers* is an extended piece of journalism exposing the illicit diamond trade in Africa. Originally published in 1957, it was Fleming's first book to be optioned, netting him £12,500 from Rank. *The Diamond Smugglers* was never made into a film, although this may not have bothered Fleming too much. Notes on the flyleaf of his own copy include a quite frank dismissal of the title, claiming: 'It is adequate journalism, but a poor book.' The children's volume is, of course, the perennial favourite *Chitty-Chitty-Bang-Bang.* 'Not a lot of people realise that he wrote that,' says Fergus.

And then there's *Talk of the Devil.* In the preface, the editors explain that in preparing this volume 'our goal has not been to assemble every overlooked scrap of Ian Fleming's writing, far less to make a definitive collection of his journalism. Instead we have tried to create a book that does justice to its author.' The editors write that the contents have been selected for rarity, for historical and biographical value, and for the glimpses they give of his opinions and enthusiasms, the overriding policy being that they should be both interesting and entertaining.

A few items have never been published; others include articles Fleming wrote during his long association with the *Sunday Times.* The editors have wisely gone back to the original typescripts, having found that some of the best lines had been attacked by over-zealous subs. 'The title is taken from a notebook in which Fleming listed names and phrases that caught his fancy. *Talk of the Devil,* which was an early contender for *Diamonds Are Forever,* caught our fancy too.'

But for the serious collector it's not so much what's in the books as what they're bound in that counts, and while the vellum (in particular) and cloth editions are classically beautiful, it's the finely bound edition that steals the show. Despite some collectors having reservations about bindings with wraparound designs leading to non-uniformity of the spines, Rob Shepherd's research into the project led him to suspect that this is what the market wanted for the fine bindings. And so Webb & Webb were commissioned: 'but we all threw in our various bits and pieces.' While works of art in themselves, the graphic imagery on the covers is quite self-explanatory although a definite aquatic theme emerges: 'Ian was very fond of the tropics and underwater life,' says Fergus. The binding of *Dr No* represents Jamaica, while several others, including *For Your Eyes Only*, *Thunderball*, and *Octopussy*, have designs depicting aspects of the underwater world that so inspired Fleming.

There are some extraordinary additions to the bindings. *Live and Let Die*, for example, has pirate treasure set into the leather on the back board. The 'pieces-of-eight' binding came about as Fergus was returning from one of Rob Shepherd's premises in Bloomsbury, and, walking down Southampton Row, caught sight of the celebrated numismatist Spink, which has been dealing in collectable coins for some three centuries. He popped in and made an enquiry. 'Yes sir,' came the reply, 'we have a pirate hoard fresh in,' and so the concept for the design of *Live and Let Die* sprouted wings. Other examples of Fergus's creative input include a diamond mounted on a scorpion's tail set into the spine of *Diamonds are Forever*.

The endpapers of the cloth sets are printed with a design based on the Fleming family's goat's head crest, and carry a facsimile of Ian Lancaster Fleming's personal book plate – complete with the family motto 'Let the deed shaw'. The endpapers for the finely bound sets is another story altogether, which by Fergus's own admission, has 'not much to do with the books, but is rather interesting.'

Fergus takes it up: 'We were in Rob's basement looking at endpapers, of which there are as many types as you can possibly imagine. Rob said, "If none of those take your fancy…" and so he clicked his fingers and an assistant emerged with a huge bale of paper that he flung on the floor.' This paper is apparently so specialised, so rare, that it is made by just one family in one small village in Japan out of the pulp of mulberry trees. They work only in winter when the water is purest and coldest. When the paper is on its frame the women of the family pick out the impurities by hand. Once it has dried it is draped over a stick and then the women come along again to polish it with camellia leaves. At this point, thinking I can see where the story is going, I interrupt with an interrogative statement: 'So that's the paper you used for the Centenary Edition endpapers, right?'

'No. No, we didn't use it in the end,' says Fergus with a laugh. 'We went for something different. I just like the story.' And with that he disappeared into snowy Curzon Street.

Of ink and ice: travels with the literary Shackleton

I'D ALWAYS PLANNED to write a column for Travels in the World of Books *about a particular hero of mine, Sir Ernest Shackleton. One of the best-known figures of the Heroic Age of Exploration, he was also something of a writer and the more I delved into his literary career, the more interesting he became. In the course of my research I interviewed the explorer's only granddaughter, the Hon. Alexandra Shackleton. She described her grandfather's literary achievements to me in such a wonderfully evocative way that it seemed a shame for me to then write one of those features where her words were repeatedly interrupted by my own editorial intrusions. So here is an edited transcription of what she told me...*

ERNEST SHACKLETON first went South on Captain Scott's *Discovery* expedition. He went because the expedition needed someone with expertise in sailing ships and grandfather had gone to sea as a sixteen-year-old in the Merchant Navy in the days of sailing ships. It was a hard life then. You had to climb 150-foot masts. The expression was, 'one hand for yourself to hold on and the other for the Queen'. The boatswain, who traditionally taught the apprentices, would beat them with the rope's end if they got it wrong. But Shackleton did so well he qualified to become a Master at the age of 24, able to command any merchant ship on the ocean.

While on *Discovery* (the National Antarctic Expedition, 1901-03) Shackleton edited *The South Polar Times*. His first expedition as leader was *Nimrod* (British Antarctic Expedition, 1907-09), which was to produce two books of note. The first was *Aurora Australis*, an anthology of writing and illustrations by the *Nimrod* expedition members that grandfather edited, and a memoir of the expedition in the form of the two-volume *The Heart of the Antarctic*, which he wrote. His third expedition was *Endurance* (Imperial Trans-Antarctic Expedition, 1914-17). In fact, the expedition comprised two ships: *Endurance* and *Aurora*. The plan was for *Endurance* in the Weddell Sea and *Aurora* in the Ross Sea. The *Endurance* shore party would cross the Antarctic via the Pole and the Ross Sea party would lay depots for them. But the expedition is informally named *Endurance* after the famous rescue mission. This was the expedition that gave rise to Shackleton's second book, *South*. During this time he wrote many letters, articles and poetry. And of course he kept a diary, often in extraordinarily harsh conditions. This may seem odd to us. I was surprised to find so many of them written in pencil, but as an archivist once explained to me, pencil lasts so much better than ink.

The South Polar Times was in three volumes and Shackleton edited two. It describes the doings of the expedition and it was illustrated brilliantly by the expedition's assistant physician, Edward Wilson. There are also cartoons of each member of the expedition. Editing The South Polar Times was very much a job after grandfather's heart: he was interested in the English language and enjoyed collecting articles, editing and trying to reflect life as it was then. It was an extraordinarily accomplished production considering it wasn't the trade of any of the men concerned. There's an edition at the National Maritime Museum that originally belonged to Rudyard Kipling and has his nameplate in it.

Of course, much of the humour of The South Polar Times has changed – what was funny then is not perhaps so funny now. The same applies to Aurora Australis, which was the first book to be printed, bound and published in Antarctica. The printers were Frank Wild and Ernest Joyce, who had taken a crash-course in how to use the press that Shackleton had acquired for the expedition. The conditions they worked in were incredibly difficult: if someone moved, then dust would settle on the page and they'd have to start all over again. People dropped pages, the ink would freeze and would have to be laboriously thawed with a candle. The binding was made up of bits of leather sledge harness and the boards themselves were made up of Venesta, a type of early plywood from the expedition's food packing cases. So you get the 'sugar edition', the 'kidney soup edition', the 'marrowbone edition' and so on. There's only one of all the editions I've seen that's plain. We don't know how many there are – certainly not more than a hundred. Only about seventy have been identified and the highest price ever paid was about £55,000. There are very few unbound copies. The Scott Polar Research Institute has got two-and-a-half copies. But if you are a collector you want a bound one.

In *Aurora* there are etchings by George Marston, the expedition artist whose nickname was 'Putty', because he was a bit fat. In those days expeditions took artists with them, a legacy from the days before photography. Grandfather took with him a photographer on the *Nimrod* expedition too, but he was nowhere near as accomplished as Frank Hurley, the photographer on the later *Endurance* expedition. My grandfather was very well aware that for an expedition to recoup costs, you had to be able to give lectures on your return, and to give lectures you had to be able to illustrate them. Otherwise how do you get the message out?

The existing copies of *Aurora* are all over the place. The British Library, Scott Polar Research Institute and so on. But the really rich collectors will 'trade up' and come to own multiple copies, keeping the best one in the bank, which I think is a cruel and wicked thing to do to a book. This applies to all polar books. When I tried unsuccessfully to buy *The South Polar Times* I was told that the person who bought it would probably keep it for best. But it was great fun bidding and I only withdrew when I had to. There's now of course a facsimile. The antiquarian book dealer John Bonham has produced a superb edition with the benefit that you can actually look at it – it's not fragile. They're all numbered and mine is Number 2.

When Shackleton returned from the *Nimrod* expedition he wrote *The Heart of the Antarctic*, a hugely evocative account in the style of the books of that era. They tell you what the men did rather than what they felt. It included fascinating shopping lists of what they bought for the expedition, including the whisky that has recently come to light under the floor of the *Nimrod* hut at Cape Royds, which I was able to visit in 2008. Also their choice of books is fascinating. There was of course a library on board *Nimrod*: the Bible and Shakespeare were a given, but there was much besides. My grandfather took poetry, of course. He was a deeply poetic man. I like his poems, although I wouldn't say that he begins to compare with someone like W.B. Yeats. I think he only wrote about five or six poems. He wrote them under the pseudonym of 'Nemo' and they're in *Aurora*. He was an accomplished writer. In fact *The Heart of the Antarctic* was so well written that it was used in schools in Holland for years, not because it was a description of a wonderful adventure, but because the English was so good.

Polar accounts today are not often noted for their quality of writing, but a century ago things were different. Scott was a good writer too, but some of the books of the time are quite difficult to get through because they're so porridgy. Writing for Shackleton came naturally, I think. He came from a family with a huge interest in literature. It was an accomplishment that in those days was often taken for granted and his style often reflected the conditions he and his men were facing. Jan Piggott in his excellent article, 'Shackleton as reader, writer and editor', mentions that, while Shackleton was capable of beautiful lyrical descriptions, when his men were under pressure his writing style becomes tighter and more muscular. But it remains incredibly evocative.

I always like Shackleton's description of when *Nimrod* set off South. They were towed by a little tug called *Koonya* to the Antarctic Circle to save coal and it was, I think, the longest tow there's ever been. It was an incredibly rough voyage and there were times when *Nimrod* could hardly see *Koonya*. Shackleton described his ship as like 'a reluctant schoolboy being dragged off to school', which is a wonderful image, don't you think?

Grandfather came back to Britain in 1909 and was knighted. He already had a Polar Medal from the *Discovery* expedition, but a bar was added, as was a further one for *Endurance*. Shackleton had two bars, but I think Frank Wild had more – I have a feeling he went on more expeditions. The Polar Medal is very special. It has a white ribbon to represent the Polar Regions and is in silver. It was silver for the officers and bronze for the men. It's awarded on the recommendation of the expedition leader at the time. That is the rule. You occasionally get discontented relatives saying that Uncle Fred should have had it, but it's meaningless because Uncle Fred wasn't given it at the time.

In between *Nimrod* and *Endurance* Shackleton tried to settle down to various business ventures, but he didn't manage it. Then, in 1911, Roald Amundsen got to the South Pole, closely followed by Scott, whose entire party tragically died on the return journey. At this time my grandfather started preparing what he regarded as the last great polar adventure: to cross the Antarctic from the Weddell Sea to the Ross Sea via the South Pole. But the Great War arrived unexpectedly and so Shackleton offered the ship and the expedition to the First Lord of the Admiralty, Winston Churchill, saying that it would be wonderful if they could all be kept together. But Churchill sent a one-word telegram, 'Proceed.' Don't forget, in those days no one thought that the war would last more than a few months. One of Shackleton's first remarks on his arrival at South Georgia was, 'When did the war end?' He was genuinely shocked to hear that the world had gone mad and there were millions dead.

Of course, *Endurance* got stuck in the ice and it was hoped that she'd rise up, but she was crushed and went down. They were in a desperate situation and nobody back home knew where they were – they might as well have been on Mars. Ernest Shackleton was always pragmatic. Obviously, as with any sailor, he grieves for the loss of his ship, but then he wrote in his diary: 'A man must set himself to a new mark, directly the old one goes.' And his new mark was to bring every member of the expedition home alive. So he called them together and told them that for the next few months they'd have to live on the ice until it broke up enough for them to take to the three little boats in order to find somewhere with a telegraph.

There they were on the ice with the Weddell Sea surging below. In some ways this was one of his greatest triumphs. He knew that people in desperate situations needed structure and routine, meals at set times and so on. Everyone shared all the jobs and there's a famous photograph of the scientists scrubbing the floors. Shackleton himself could do any job on the expedition, however menial, and did. Birthdays were celebrated. There were football games, dog races, amateur theatricals, and all the time Shackleton was watching his men, getting to know them, which was not typical for leaders at that time. For instance, he didn't say, 'You, you and you, go in this tent.' He balanced the personalities, and the most difficult people he put in his own tent.

Eventually, one of the members of the ship's company who was prone to seasickness – Thomas Orde-Lees – felt slightly queasy and noticed that the ice was moving. By this time they'd decided that the nearest land was Elephant Island. It was difficult to decide when to go: too soon and they'd be crushed by the ice, too late and the ice would break up under the tents and they'd all drown. The journey to Elephant Island was a complete nightmare: some of the men were half-dead by the time they got there.

It's a deeply disagreeable place, Elephant Island. I've flown over it. Effectively it's a rocky mountain-top sticking out from the ocean. There were penguins and seals for food, but these would migrate and grandfather was reluctant to lay up stock. After a few days he took the decision that they had to go to South Georgia, the nearest place that wind and tide would allow. So he took five companions, decked up the biggest of the boats – the *James Caird* – and set sail. It was an incredible gamble. If Frank Worsley, the *Endurance* captain, hadn't been such an incredible navigator they'd have missed South Georgia, never to be seen again. Shackleton left Wild, his trusty second in command, in charge of the remaining twenty-two men on Elephant Island.

Worsley said two interesting things about the boat journey. He wrote that, however bad things were, Shackleton made his men think that things would get better. He knew there was no rationale behind this, but it seems to me that giving people something beyond themselves to believe in is the essence of leadership. Worsley also wrote that Shackleton kept an eagle eye on everyone, and if any man was failing he ordered hot milk, not just for him but for everybody, so that this man would not feel he was the only one not coping.

They drew near South Georgia. They could see South Georgia, but a hurricane arose and they had to stand off to prevent being dashed on the rocks. By that stage they were suffering appallingly from thirst and their tongues were black and swollen. And then at last they made landfall and there was a little stream, and they had the most wonderful drink they'd ever had, and they ate baby albatrosses. They were too weak to pull up the boat properly, so Shackleton took the longest watch and stood there holding the painter while the boat ebbed and flowed. The next day they put the boat somewhere safer and set about climbing South Georgia, because of course they were on the wrong side of the island if they wanted to get to the whaling station of Stromness. There were no communications at Stromness, but from there it was possible to get a ship to the Falkland Islands, where there were communications. As they crossed the island, they thought they felt the presence of an extra man. There's a line in T.S. Eliot's 'The Waste Land' – 'Who is the third who walks always beside you?' – that refers to this.

This story of the *James Caird* and how his men were all eventually rescued is in grandfather's second book, *South*. Of course, he didn't actually write *South*: he had an amanuensis, Edward Saunders. Shackleton wanted to put Saunders' name on the cover, but Saunders refused. It was very painful for grandfather to relive the story, especially of the ship sinking, but they said they must go on because they needed the story. It was published in 1919 and it was much more of a rush-job than *The Heart of the Antarctic*; and unfortunately it wasn't published on very good paper, which is why it's gone brown. Because of the war and various restrictions there was no good paper available. You can always tell the early editions this way.

Shackleton started a fourth expedition – *Quest* (the Shackleton-Rowett Expedition, 1921) – and he got as far as South Georgia. There's a wonderful last entry in his diary at the Scott Polar Research Institute in which he writes: 'in the glimmering twilight a lone star hovers gem-like over the bay.' He didn't know he was dying and so that makes it doubly poetic.

Grandfather could recite pages and pages of poetry. There's a nice description of when he was on *Discovery* with Hugh Robert Mill, who was in fact grandfather's first biographer and a lifelong friend. Apparently Mill was quite disconcerted about how much poetry this young officer knew and wrote in his diary: 'such literary absorption savours of the impractical'. He changed his mind, though.

From their childhood the Shackletons would learn pages of poetry by heart and would identify quotations over dinner. He loved Robert Browning. 'Prospice' was one of his favourite poems: 'For sudden the worst turns the best to the brave.'

Index